THE
DOORPRENEUR

Copyright © 2019 Tony LeBlanc

All rights reserved. No part of this publication may be reproduced, distributed, or transmitted in any form or by any means, including photocopying, recording, or other electronic or mechanical methods, without the prior written permission of the publisher, except in the case of brief quotations embodied in critical reviews and certain other noncommercial uses permitted by copyright law. For permission requests, write to the publisher, addressed "Attention: Permissions Coordinator," at the address below.

Open Door Publishing Ltd
813 Champlain Street, Unit 6
Dieppe, NB E1A 9P1

Send feedback to books@doorpreneur.com

ISBN: 978-1-9991794-0-3 (print)
ISBN: 978-1-9991794-1-0 (ebook)

Ordering Information:

Special discounts are available on quantity purchases by corporations, associations, and others. For details, contact books@doorpreneur.com.

THE DOORPRENEUR

PROPERTY MANAGEMENT BEYOND THE RENT ROLL

Tony LeBlanc

CONTENTS

1. Stop Changing Lightbulbs—Change Your Life!....................1
2. Property Management Reimagined—Why Now Matters ...11
3. Property Managers—Real Estate's True Entrepreneurs........19
4. It's Time for Purposeful Work 37
5. How Do I Become a Doorpreneur?......................................49
6. The Art and Science of Property Management....................61
7. Value Is the Key 75
8. Growth—The Foundation of the Doorpreneur Model 85
9. Technology and The Reinvention of Property Management 95
10. Grow Every Day..107
11. Invest in YOU!..117
12. The Meaning of Success 127

CHAPTER 1

STOP CHANGING LIGHTBULBS
CHANGE YOUR LIFE!

Consider this: You can learn a lot about people from what they drop in the hallways of their apartment buildings. There are places where people toss crumpled food wrappers and beer cans on the floor, mistaking the building for a garbage can. Then there are buildings where hallways are pristine and seasonal wreaths and welcome signs hang on the doors.

These markers tell us that residential property management is special because we aren't just dealing with buildings. We're handling something far more sensitive: people and their homes, from single-family units and duplexes to small buildings and skyscrapers with hundreds of apartments.

A lot of property managers forget this truth amid the monthly hustle-and-bustle of business. The task of checking off our to-do lists is in full swing and we lose sight of our true priorities. But we shouldn't.

HOMES ARE THE BACKDROPS OF OUR LIVES

In 2013, my company managed about 1,240 units with more than 2,000 tenants. I remember thinking even then that the spectrum of people whom we touch on a daily basis is so incredible. We share some of our tenants' best and worst experiences—life, death, marriage, divorce, and everything in between.

Some of our tenants are students preparing for their life's work. It's a time of great memories, and we get to be part of their experience. How terrific is that?

We also have new couples moving in together for the first time. We all know how "interesting" this development can be as we get to know a person and reach new levels of trust, love, and appreciation. These relationships are built within the four walls of the homes we provide, and that is tremendous, too.

These are the places where families are created and childhood memories made. How can we not see this business as anything but special? We need to be proud of what we do. It matters.

PROPERTY MANAGEMENT IS A TOUGH BUSINESS

Most property managers don't share my perspective on the industry. It may surprise you, too, to view property management as a means to creating wealth, finding your purpose, and establishing a business empire. But that's how I see it. It's a tough job but also one of the most rewarding!

You have to have a pretty thick skin in order to be able to deal with some of the situations that happen on a daily basis. You need to remember an incredible amount of details and be ready to take immediate action at a moment's notice. It's a process-heavy industry with many things that have to be done each and every month. The job can be a grinding, merciless routine.

The reality is that when your phone rings, it's rarely good news or someone on the other line waiting to praise you or your company. You have to keep a lot of people happy, namely your tenants and property owners. Then there are your team members, because you couldn't accomplish anything without them. The never-ending stress wears most people down. In fact, the average amount of time someone lasts in property management is 18 months. Because of those complexities and many others, the property management industry hasn't been given enough credit for the fantastic opportunities it presents to someone like you and me.

For the most part, all you hear are the negative sides of our industry, and I think I know why: Bad news and photos of trashed apartments get people's attention. But if all you see or hear are stories about slumlords and disreputable tenants, why would you have any other opinion about the industry?

The other issue that gives property management a bad name is its financial structure. Property managers consider themselves on the low end of most real estate transactions compared to what realtors make in commissions. The sale of a property contrasted with monthly and yearly management fees is not going to look good, and can lead you down a path of resentment.

That said, the idea of investing in real estate is exciting, and it's safe to say that most real estate investors love the acquisition process. It's fun and very sexy. Most property managers also are investors and very familiar with the dopamine rush of buying real estate.

The onboarding of a new property may feel like a punch list that needs to be checked off, but once we've been awarded the management contract, there's a short period of time when it's exciting to see the new income coming in and to feel the prestige of having a certain property in our portfolio.

From the property manager's perspective, the overall sentiment also can be that we are working to build someone else's net worth and not our own. Everything we charge to a property is an expense to the property owner. By making money in the management firm, we essentially affect the potential returns for our investors. We sometimes feel guilty about our pricing models and additional fees that we have to charge, but we sometimes forget we also are running a business and to run a business, one must be profitable.

It's up to us to embrace property management as a great profession. You don't hear doctors complain about their work the way we do, and if they did, who would want to work with them?

In other words, property management has a bad rap because we allow it to have a bad rap. We are the problem, and we are the solution. If we start to collectively see and treat the business as a great business, others will see it as a great business. It's that simple.

So why on earth would I write a book suggesting you should get into the business?

First, I believe this industry's time has come. The changing demographics across North America, coupled with cultural and lifestyle trends, make that clear. Second, property management itself is on the brink of change, too, and with that change will come newfound respect for the industry as a vital creator of wealth and happiness.

Finally, I am convinced from my own personal experience that property management is as an affordable way to get started in business and a strong foundation for a diversified and thriving portfolio. In other words, it's the successful route to becoming a Doorpreneur.

WHAT'S A DOORPRENEUR?

From a very early age, as I watched my mother run a property management company, I believed it was a fantastic foundation on which to build a business empire. It's not about changing light bulbs. It's about changing lives!

I do the job differently than most people, and that's why I coined the term "Doorpreneur." This book will show you how to become one, too.

Whether you like it or not, property management is a niche market and a service-based business that caters specifically to real estate investors. In most cases, our target market is local. As a property manager, you have only one group of clients from whom you earn most of your profits (the property owners) and a fixed number of assets you can control (your market share).

A Doorpreneur is someone who can take that existing property management business and grow it beyond the rent roll. In short, they use the management firm as a springboard to establish an entire business network.

Most management firms are essentially mom-and-pop shops, managing fewer than 300 units or "doors." It's still rare to find management firms that manage more than 1,000 units and even rarer to find firms with multiple locations. Knowing this is critical if you dare to dream big and want to grow past your rent rolls.

What if there was a way you could take what you do and what you know, pack up your trained team, and face a much larger client base? What if you could take your services directly to the general public and not just real estate investors?

That's the secret game changer!

The Doorpreneur model is twofold: You must first create a property management experience that is second to none. It must be dialed in and producing profits before you contemplate growth in different verticals. I also recommend that you grow it to a point to where you either think you have as many units as you would want to manage or you've hit a limit within your market.

When that's accomplished, you can create a secondary business unit that services your current management properties. Great examples are landscaping, snow removal, maintenance, and cleaning.

Once you've established this new venture and proven its viability, you can deploy the ultimate strategy of expanding this new business unit to the general public. By doing that, you are no longer restrained by the limitations of your core property management firm or even the limits of the rental properties in the communities you serve. The world is yours.

You can market yourself and close deals beyond the realm of the average property manager, transforming yourself into the new serial entrepreneur known as the Doorpreneur.

If you're in the business of property management, this book is for you. It will show you the potential of our industry and how to build your own empire. If you aren't yet a property manager, but you have an idea that purchasing a rental property and managing it could be a means of augmenting your income, then this book also is for you. It will show you the potential of creating wealth through wise property management.

If you already are an entrepreneur and are eager to find the means to grow your business, this book also will be an important guide. It will show you the way to accomplish your goals, using property management as your base.

WALKING THE WALK, TALKING THE TALK

Up until the age of 16, my mother and I lived in an apartment building where she was the resident manager. I made myself useful when it came to maintenance, and the chore I remember most vividly was cleaning the hallways. They seemed to go on forever. Each Saturday or Sunday, I knew I had what it seemed at the time to be agonizing work waiting for me. During the winter months, it was even worse. Lots of snow and salt was often tracked into the building and made the cleaning that much harder.

Looking back, I consider this to be the birthplace of my work ethic. It taught me an important lesson about what it takes to keep a building clean and tenants and property owners happy. As a tenant myself, I felt empowered walking into a clean building that smelled good because I had done the work to make it happen.

My mother sometimes had to deal with people who were upset for one reason or another, but she never lost her cool. In fact, it seemed to me everyone loved my mother. If you had told me then that I would one day be following in her footsteps and managing more than 2,000 apartments across three cities, I would have chided you for making a joke and kept on cleaning. If you had further suggested I would use property management as the means to grow a larger business empire, I would have laughed uproariously. But life has a way of unfolding in ways we never can imagine.

I never considered my childhood apartment as a temporary place to sleep and eat while I waited to have a "real" home one day. It *was* my home. We weren't wealthy, but I never lacked any of life's essentials. I had a happy childhood with lots of friends, and from an early age, I liked nothing better than to play outside and stay active. Although I helped my mother and learned the basics of the business at a young age, I still had time to be a kid.

I was 16 years old when mother saved enough money to buy her first home. While it was lovely to see her as a property owner, I'd had a happy childhood in our apartment. It wasn't until after I embraced property management as a career years later that I really saw its business potential.

Over the past 10 years, I did what it took to become a Doorpreneur. I started a management company from nothing—and grew it into a group of companies of which I'm extremely proud. I've used property management to support my family, as my mother did, and to provide wealth for my clients, a home for tenants, and a way to have a more satisfying and flexible life for myself.

I'll show you how to do it, too.

NEXT STEPS

Assess your attitude. The road to change begins with an understanding of where you are now so you will know when you reach your destination. Consider how you feel about property management: Do you see it as an ugly stepson of the real estate industry? Is it merely a means to survive or perhaps a side job? Would you like to explore it further?

Assess your industry knowledge. If you're not in the business, what do you think it involves? If you were to purchase a rental property, would you try to manage it yourself or hire a manager? What qualities would you expect them to have? If you already are a property manager, can you imagine its potential? Are you interested in exploring property management as a way to change the entire way you do business?

CHAPTER 2

PROPERTY MANAGEMENT REIMAGINED
WHY NOW MATTERS

Children don't look up at the stars at night and wistfully tell their parents that they'd love to manage rental properties when they grow up. They don't see our business with the heart-stirring drama ignited by thoughts of being a doctor or a veterinarian. They don't yearn to develop a new strain of management agreement clauses in their science lab or touch people's hearts with a novel about a handsome property manager with superpowers.

The upshot is that property management doesn't appeal to people as a sexy profession and there's some truth to that. It's an incredibly difficult business with demands bombarding you from all sides. Unlike most businesses with one kind of client, property management has two: owners and tenants.

The building owner wants your help to create wealth and protect his or her investment. They hire you to collect the rent, maintain the building, and manage all aspects of running the property. You are the single most important person to help them accomplish what they need to do, but they don't always treat your role with that in mind.

The tenant wants a comfortable, safe, and well-maintained space in which they can live virtually hassle free. You're the person who makes that happen, but sometimes you would never guess that by their tone. While many people are warm, friendly, and responsive to working cooperatively with you, others can be extremely difficult.

News and social media reports of horribly maintained buildings and callous rent collectors abound, while the day-to-day operations of most property managers who build supportive relationships with clients are rarely told. We're considered the real estate world's side business, and most people are believed to have fallen into property management by mistake, not by choice.

GENERATIONAL SHIFTS

Lifestyle changes are propelling growth in our industry as more and more people in Canada and the US seek to rent rather than own housing. Two key factors are fueling this cultural shift: the aging of the baby boomer generation and the rise of young millennials.

Baby boomers, who were born between 1946 and 1965, comprise 9.6 million Canadians, according to 2011 census data. That means that about three of every 10 Canadians are baby boomers and they will represent 23 percent of the population by 2031 compared to 15 percent in 2011. Meanwhile, the US Census Bureau estimates that more than 29 percent of Americans will be over 65 by 2029.

The aging generation in both countries means there is a growing demand for smaller housing units such as apartments or condominium units, especially in walkable neighborhoods. Baby boomers who opt to stay in their own homes, meanwhile, want to purchase additional services to help make that possible, setting the stage for the spin-off companies of your property management business.

Millennials are the other significant population pushing change in the housing market. Representing 9.8 million people in Canada, they are the largest segment of the nation's population and will dominate trends in the foreseeable future.

Similarly, there are just over 75 million millennials in the US, making them the largest generation in the nation's history. They tend to marry, have children, and become homeowners later in life, according to a report by the Urban Institute, a think tank in Washington, DC. The rate of millennial homeownership in the US was 37 percent in 2015, about 8 percent lower than the homeownership rate of Generation Xers and baby boomers at the same age.

The report suggests that if the home ownership rate for millennials had stayed the same as previous generations, there would be about 3.4 million more homeowners in the US today. In addition, millennials are heavily focused on the so-called "sharing economy," and as a result, they're comfortable living in apartment buildings in expensive city centers where they can walk to work and to places to meet friends. They're less keen on purchasing a home in the suburbs, even when they begin earning a regular income.

Also, in the current "gig economy" of temporary or freelance work, millennials often feel their income is not secure and so are less inclined to want to make long-term commitments like purchasing a home.

They don't even want to be tied to a specific geographic area because they want to explore the world between gigs, and they leave not sure if they'll want to come back.

Taken together, these trends fuel a growing demand for apartments and that, in turn, means a growing need for good property managers. How significant is the potential growth? You need only to look overseas.

Consider: Nearly 31 percent (namely, one-third) of Australians live in rental properties, according to 2016 Australian Bureau of Statistics census figures and a special report prepared by IBIS World on Australian Market Research.

Property managers manage most of these rental households on behalf of landlords, and revenues from the property management industry for 2017-2018 were estimated to reach $3.4 billion with 25,012 employees. Given similar trends, there's no reason that can't happen here in North America.

That's not to say there are no obstacles. Because there are no specific training requirements or licenses required to enter the industry in most of Canada and in some areas of the United States, many people start without the knowledge they need to make it work as a viable business.

While they may be very successful managing one small unit, if they lack business experience and a reliable team, it doesn't take long for problems to mount. And as Canada and the United States become renters' nations, the level of skill and professionalism needed to manage properties will grow, too.

Today's property manager needs to go into the business with the same planning and preparation required for any other challenging enterprise. When you have that, you have the opportunity to reinvent the rental experience for a new generation of renters and reinvent the ownership experience for investors.

More training programs are necessary, along with industry leaders willing to share their innovations in every aspect of the business from marketing to development. We also need to use new technology to help us run our businesses more efficiently.

To make it work for you, you need a solid business strategy and skill set and the belief that you can create the foundation of a wealth-creating initiative. When you have that, you can succeed as a Doorpreneur.

IT'S ABOUT MORE THAN DOORS

If you walk into virtually any property management conference in the world, "How many doors do you manage?" would seem to be the only question that matters. The more doors you have, the better off you appear.

Door count is the amount of properties or units within a larger property you currently have under management. Don't get me wrong, door count is very important, but it's not an accurate way to judge the profitability or success of a management company. The door count will give you some pretty good insights as to what a day in the life looks like for a property manager because it involves staff levels and revenues, among other facets of the business, but it's only one piece of a much larger puzzle. I've seen companies in the red managing thousands of units, and I've also seen a guy who manages 100 doors make a fortune.

To build a sustainable and profitable business, I believe that you need to have multiple streams of income and not rely solely on management fees. Having worked with IBM for almost 15 years as a software consultant, I've had diversification instilled in me from day one.

My journey in property management started just like many other people. My eyes were focused on the management fees. Since I was not a licensed realtor, the sales part never really came into the picture until almost 10 years later. I earned a few other fees charged for miscellaneous items but management fees were the bulk of the income.

After some time, I quickly realized that management fees alone were not producing enough profits to sustain the workload so we introduced leasing fees to help us lease units faster as well as provide another stream of income.

The mindset of thinking that door count is the "be-all and end-all" is where the problem lies. Most property management companies are on the smaller scale. Let's take about 500 units as an example. If you keep going back to these 500 units every year looking to create "new" fees, you will eventually hit a wall. Either the owners of the properties will fire you because you're too expensive or you'll simply run out of fees to charge.

Consistently charging new fees to the same doors is not the solution to growth. This will eventually have the opposite effect. In order for real growth to happen, the mindset shift needs to occur.

The real growth occurs when you can discover opportunities in your management portfolio that have enough promise to be taken to the general public.

Once I became known for having a healthy and reputable property management company, I could press the ignition on my ultimate business plan, which meant creating new brands and businesses to complement what I had already built.

Step by step, company-by-company, I am growing, expanding, and sharing my experience to reinvent property management. With each success and failure, I am more inspired than ever to keep moving along the unique track of Doorpreneurship. Since I cleaned that first hallway and bought my first triplex, I understood there was potential for a much bigger and more important play in the property management field.

It's not all about toilets, tenants, and trouble.

It's about people, properties, and profits.

If you can begin to see this vision, too, I promise that you will never look at property management the same way. To adopt the Doorpreneur mindset, you have to be aware of all the opportunities associated with managing properties. If I can build and grow it, so can you.

NEXT STEPS

Consider the image of property management in your community. Whether you are working in the field or not, do you have an open mind about improving the image or at least clarifying the public's perception of property managers? What single step would you recommend to improve the industry's image?

Investigate your market. In your community, do you see signs of increased activity with new rental properties? How does the number of apartments now compare to 10 years ago? What apartment projects have been announced or are currently under construction? Are there opportunities for you to get involved in their management?

CHAPTER 3

PROPERTY MANAGERS
REAL ESTATE'S TRUE ENTREPRENEURS

Who would I have to become in order to manage 100, 500, 5000 or even 50,000 doors?

I found myself asking this question a few years back. "Who do I need to become to open a second location?" I wondered. I was beyond scared, and excuses raced through my head: I can't open up another location. I have too much work to do here. I don't have time to deal with an entire new team. I don't even know how to start getting the process going!

For most of us, these thoughts can be enough to prevent us from reaching new levels in our journey of self-discovery. We get consumed with the unknowns to the extent that we are no longer able to make any forward progress and the dream dies inside of us. What differentiates some people from others is their ability to take the leap of faith with a belief in themselves that is so strong that nothing can stop them.

Most property managers don't ask—or don't want to ask—themselves what it would take for *them* to get to the next level. I would go a step further in saying that most have never asked themselves the question because I've been around the management industry long enough to see what it can do to people.

A lot of management companies are on the smaller size with fewer than 500 doors. This makes for an environment that is very owner-centric. What I mean by that is that the owner still is the main person running all aspects of the business from sales to marketing, leasing, maintenance, HR, and everything in between.

When you're bogged down by day-to-day activities as a manager, it's hard to find time to look up to try and plan ahead.

ENTREPRENEURIAL PERSONALITIES

A business owner's personality tends to fall into one of three categories:

- The Entrepreneur, who dares to dream big
- The Technician, the worker
- The Manager, who looks at numbers and performance

It's very hard to be all three of these personalities, which are the foundation of Michael Gerber's *The E-Myth Revisited* book series. Most of us just don't have the ability to be competent in every area so we tend to revert to what we do best. Gerber's book was the first book I ever read on business, and it changed my working life.

It's a good idea for every property manager to read *The E-Myth Revisited* because it demonstrates the values and responsibilities of each of these three personality types, and it ties very nicely into the world of property management.

For instance, one of the most important traits of a great entrepreneurial mind is constant growth, and learning something new every day is one of my daily rituals. My morning "power hour" is without a doubt one of the most important strategies I've deployed to grow my business and, more important, myself.

Most people enter the management world with the best of intentions. From my point of view, the entry point into property management typically occurs for three reasons:

- **Family businesses.** You took over what your parents started.
- **Accidental landlords.** You somehow fell into management and wound up liking it.
- **Real estate agencies.** You're a realtor who gets into the business, either by accident or on purpose, to supplement your income.

Regardless of how you got into the business, you must see it through an entrepreneurial perspective. And, of course, you'll start the journey with the same fears, anxiety, enthusiasm, and excitement as any other entrepreneur when they start a new business.

The first step for newly formed management companies is that they have to get doors. This is obvious. A property management company cannot survive if it does not have properties to manage. The problem is that most people stop at just managing properties and not seeing the greater opportunities around them.

There's nothing wrong with managing doors and doing nothing else. But for those who dare to dream, the path to becoming a Doorpreneur is the ultimate goal. A thriving property management business has one or more complementary businesses that serve its portfolio as well as the general public. Serial entrepreneurs like myself salivate at the thought of these untapped markets because they not only represent the wave of the future but your way to a new life.

PROPERTY MANAGEMENT MUST BE PROFITABLE

The most important attribute of a successful entrepreneur is their ability to create profits. Profits are what keep a business running and growing. A lack of financial responsibility is one of the biggest challenges facing our industry. In fact, the average profit margin is 6 percent, according to Jordan Muela of the *Profitable Property Management* podcast.

This is very disturbing to hear but it makes sense. If property management is one of the toughest jobs out there and it barely turns a profit, is there any wonder why it has such a high turnover rate and unflattering image?

A successful industry is often associated with healthy profits. I don't think anyone can argue that. Just look at realtors. They're very well paid and are looked at in a completely different light then property managers.

There are several reasons why a management company or any other business for that matter can fail, and poor profitability is one reason. A management company must be able to sustain itself. As the business grows, other expenses follow. And if your margins are too tight, you could get in trouble quickly.

One of the most damaging practices in the management world is when a management company also is involved in sales. This means that they are also licensed realtors. Often, the management fees will be deeply discounted in order to get a sale because the sales bring in big commissions.

Do you see the problem?

Property management is being positioned from the start as a less-than-worthy service—so much so that some people sometimes can get management fees to almost nothing. This is a quick way to run a management division into the ground and should be avoided at all costs. We need the exact opposite to happen.

Management will be the part of the transaction that maintains the longest relationships as it involves the most time and energy. We need to make sure that this is very clear and to stick to our guns when it comes to fees. It should not be a loss leader for sales.

Another practice that hurts our ability to turn a good profit is when large property owners decide to start managing properties for others. Because they already have the infrastructure and are known for owning rentals, people naturally ask if they would be interested in managing their properties.

They think that if the money they make from third-party properties helps them take care of their stuff, that's enough, and they're happy. Profits are a secondary thought. This practice is sabotaging our industry because it's used as a means to another end. This is bad for the industry because it affects our pricing model.

It sends the message that our services are not worth anything if we negate the value of what goes into managing a property. How on earth can an industry clear its name of a negative public image and increase its stock if we, as property managers and owners, don't put a meaningful value on our work?

It's a problem—and a big one.

Most people who get into property management are not thinking that it can be something special and entrepreneurial.

Take realtors as an example. They come into the business with such excitement and pride. They tell everyone in the world to contact them if they have something to buy or sell. They go on about the money, the lifestyle it provides, and all the perks. On the flip side, I don't think I've ever heard those same sentiments from newbies in the property management world. (Well, maybe I've seen it from one person…me.)

Property management is its own entity and should be successfully established before you expand into other ventures. Your rent roll should produce great profits for its shareholders as well as provide great service to clients and team members. Trying to grow another arm of the business will be painful if this is not accomplished first.

Property management can provide great profit margins when done properly. I see a lot of people, including myself at times, discount their services just to get business. They say to themselves that they will recover from the shortfall with other service offerings. From experience, I know this can lead you down a dark hole of misery.

The 80/20 rule is alive and well in the management world. That means 80 percent of your time will be eaten up with 20 percent of your clients. In addition, this 20 percent are almost always the ones who also pay the least.

I have this exact problem in my business today. We have one client for whom we manage five buildings with a total of about 85 units. The properties have high turnover, lower-end tenants, and need a lot of maintenance. In addition, the owners always want to do things quickly and cheaply. Listen, I'm all for cost-effectiveness but not at the price of failing to properly fix something once and then paying double the amount to fix it several months later.

That's one of the reasons why creating a great management company takes time. It rarely happens overnight. You'll learn from your mistakes, and eventually you'll become laser focused on the clients with whom you want to work and the types of properties you want to manage. Once you become a Doorpreneur, you can include the potential upside of other lines of business. But when you're starting out, you must focus on the profitability of the management contracts alone.

Follow this one rule and you'll save yourself a lot of headaches down the road.

MY ENTREPRENEURIAL JOURNEY

I've always had a side hustle, and by the time I hit 30, I was involved in more than five different businesses. I excelled in each but never quit my full-time job as a technical consultant. The entrepreneurial spirit burned inside of me, even while I depended on a salary to support my family.

Wealth has always intrigued me. Not so much in terms of money but in terms of the power that it can provide and the doors it can open. People with wealth and what looked like carefree lifestyles intrigued me. I wanted my own money, and I knew I had to earn it.

My first real experience as an entrepreneur was in the nutritional supplement industry. I was a bodybuilder at the time, and I was introduced into a network marketing business. Like a lot of people out there, I had no idea what network marketing was. I was young, full of energy, and wanted to get into something that made me feel as though I was part of something special. It gave me exactly that.

I had been taking the company's supplements and loved them before I joined the business. I quickly became very active and had some immediate success. Over time, I became their top salesperson and was having a great time. Aside from earning a bit of money on the side, I was building up my entrepreneurial chops, as they say. Every day was an opportunity to either sell some products, recruit other salespeople, or cultivate new relationships with supplement stores.

After a year or so, the company went out of business. Luckily, I had created a great relationship with their manufacturer and, with their blessing, I decided to rebrand the product under my own name. I kept it simple with a protein powder and creatine mixture; it tasted horrible, but boy, did it ever work! My friend and I partnered on the enterprise, which started as The Supplement Guys and then I rebranded on my own as TSG Nutrition.

It was a good product for me because, as a bodybuilder, I was familiar with how it worked. I had a lot of friends who were interested in it, and I called all the gyms to get them to sell it for me. That was the first time I had to find the courage to do cold calls. It taught me a lot, and we kept the business going for several years.

My second biggest venture into entrepreneurship was in financial planning and life insurance. I learned an entirely new set of skills and some valuable lessons from this part of my life. First, I had to get my life insurance license. I was scared to death of this exam because it involved a new skill set that was vastly different from my previous experience. Preparing for this exam was one of the most difficult things I had done in my professional career. I just threw myself into it, wound up passing the exam, and did quite well in the business.

This was the first time when I almost left my full-time job in order to pursue another business to the next level. Thankfully, I didn't because the life insurance company closed down within a couple of years. I could have gone out on my own, but looking back, I'm very happy about how things turned out.

I had a technician's mindset in parts of my day job, but in my side hustle, I was all entrepreneur. I worked "on" my businesses not just "in" them. I envisioned each new business in its entirety and then broke it down into its parts. It was at this stage in my life I also developed the business philosophies that were to guide me to even greater success when I later went into property management.

There were three things in particular that I instinctively did differently from other people:

First, I saw that if I could produce the right results for my customers, everything else would follow, including the profits. I put customers first every time, and I still do. As a property manager, some people think their focus has to be the property owner, but it pays off if you focus on the tenants and produce the right results for *them*.

Second, I defined the future of each business and then I calibrated it to the present. If the two didn't align, I went about changing what was happening in the business to keep it on track.

Third, I always have meaning in my work. Work is not just a series of problems to be solved—it has to create something worthwhile. In my management company, I am not just having backed-up toilets fixed, snow removed, or lawns mowed. I am enhancing the lives of thousands of people.

I am still grateful that I spent a decade and a half with IBM, but I always knew that I was meant to do something on my own. It wasn't until a friend casually suggested that I return to my roots and property management that I saw it as the logical next step in my evolution as an entrepreneur. It made perfect sense.

GROUND FLOOR PROPERTY MANAGEMENT

By then, my family had expanded to two children, and I had moved back to my hometown in eastern Canada. In January 2010, I founded Ground Floor Property Management Inc. It all started with a duplex on Spurr Street in Moncton, New Brunswick. Within a month, I had another 25 units.

I also still worked full time as a software consultant and within three months, I was up to managing 100 units simply through word of mouth. The company my mother worked for was not taking smaller clients so they were sent my way. Once I hit the 100-door mark, I knew I could not sustain the pace while working a full-time job.

I also knew that I needed help if I was going to get this company where I envisioned it. I called my mother, who had more than 30 years of experience in the business, and I asked her advice about how I should move forward. I knew who would help me take the company to the next level. It just happened that he worked for my mother for almost 20 years!

Stephen and I had known each other for some time, and I invited him to my home to share my thoughts on partnering up in a management company. I think we both knew pretty quickly that we would be a great team. I'm very pleased to report that Stephen and I are still partners to this day, and I could not see myself doing what I'm doing with anyone else.

When you are growing a business and you need help, you don't want someone just like yourself. If you are a dreamer and big picture person, you need to partner with a technician. I knew I needed Stephen at my side because he was well versed in handling all the day-to-day details, and I could focus on what I loved, which was sales and growing the company.

Almost 10 years later, we still complement each other extremely well. I'm still the entrepreneur, and he's still the textbook technician (another *E-Myth* term). We manage more than 2000 doors across three provinces, and we've experienced just about every property management scenario imaginable.

The thing about both myself and my partner is that we are both willing and able to go out and do just about anything we would ask our 50 team members to do. For example, it's not uncommon for one of us to show up at apartments to do move-in or move-out inspections and deal with tenant issues. We'll pick up a paintbrush and help clean. We know that by leading through example, it gives us a lot more credibility with our maintenance staff, leasing agents, and business partners.

We were determined to raise the stakes on professionalism and service in our industry, and we have never stopped trying to do more. I've had no choice but to grow or else I would never have been able to pull off what I did.

FROM ZERO TO INFINITY

The barrier to entry in the management world is very low where I live in Canada. There are no license requirements so anyone can put up a sign and call themselves a property manager.

It took me a year from jumping into property management to sign my first management contract. I could have done things more quickly, but I wanted to carefully build the business because I had a strong feeling that it was going to be my future.

I was also faced with some start-up issues that were new to me—specifically marketing and branding. It was very important to me to create brand messaging that was beautiful and polished. A local marketing firm helped me flush out my ideas and create some great visuals that gave me a huge leg up when I eventually launched the business.

The entire start-up process cost me around $15,000, most of it which went into branding assets such as logos, a website, and some copywriting, and I was fortunate to have a good job to pay for it. The other most important aspect of this start-up phase was nailing down our market position. Our original tag line read: "Clarify the Unknowns, Simplify Your Investments." This rings true today and still makes me smile.

Despite the slow run-up, we grew the company very quickly, hitting 1,000 units within our first three years. This was both a blessing and a curse. It put us in fight-or-flight mode a lot as we confronted challenges and demands from all sides.

All stages of business growth represent pressure points. In property management, for example, the start-up phase ranges up to 100 units. In that phase, it is pretty much a one-person show. Growing the business at that phase is not as difficult as you might think. If you are known in the real estate world and word gets out, you'll get a lot of calls. There may be many people in the business but there are not many *good* people in it. If you do a great job from the outset, your star keeps rising. You might outsource your maintenance work in this phase because you still don't have enough work to hire a full-time person.

Phase Two is managing from 100 to 250 units. That's when things start to get real. You generally have to take a big leap of faith and shift full time into your business. It's frightening because you still aren't sure how things are going to work out. You are likely to hire a full-time maintenance person. By the time you hit 150 units, you start looking for a full-time administrator. It's reckoning day when you realize you can't handle all the calls, showings, lease signings, and other issues. That's when you look for someone who can handle administrative details and has some accounting knowledge.

Up to 250 units and you are likely still working out of your home. Now it's time to invest in an office if you want your growth to continue, although you can run a good size management business virtually. This stage can be painful as you feel the pressure mounting because now you have two salaries to pay and the possible overhead of an office.

Phase Three is 250 to 500 units, and it involves hiring a second full-time maintenance person and a bookkeeper to ensure that all the bills get paid. This is a tricky phase when any weaknesses in your system will become obvious. Your bills mount with things like workers' compensation, liability insurance, gas allowances, office supplies, cell phones, and payroll. At the same time, you start to feel successful because you aren't constantly running after business—some of it starts to find you.

By Phase Four (500 to 1000 units), you may need as many as 10 to 20 full-time staff to make it work, including two to three property managers and a full-time accountant. You need to deal with sick leaves, vacations, and employee issues. At the start of the phase, profits dip again because of the increase in expenses and then they level out. Staffing is a constant issue and it needs to be monitored at all times, especially as you move up the ladder of big business. You are more and more removed from renting units and dealing with tenants.

Now is a good time to think about what you have learned about your business and how it could be diversified to add other streams of income. You may shudder at the thought of starting other businesses, but you also notice that you have a large and flexible staff and the ability to obtain more contracts in other areas. This is when it's time to develop the mindset of the Doorpreneur.

EXPAND YOUR VIEW AND YOUR OPTIONS

The secret is to broaden your perspective as soon as you control an asset. It can be a single-family home, a large multi-family apartment building, a small linear mall, or a large office building. When you control an asset, you have options. Becoming a Doorpreneur is not about managing properties and then creating businesses just to make money on everything else. Instead, it first requires you to build something special within the property management space.

It all becomes a game of trust and transparency. If you have done well for people on the property management side of things, they will be open to discussing other ways for you to provide services. Running a professional property management business is the best foundation to gain the trust of others and be able to explore expanding opportunities.

I started a landscaping business, for example. You could start a snow removal firm if you live in a cold climate. You could siphon off trained staff into a cleaning company. Or, you could begin to offer maintenance contracts to buildings you don't manage but you know need monthly help. Every step you take adds pressure, but pressure is what produces power. If you want to build your business empire, you need to be willing to confront it and come up with solutions.

I made the decision over and over again to step into the pressure instead of avoiding it. For instance, our company, CORE Property Care, offers maintenance and other services to commercial and residential buildings. We deal not only with our management properties but also with the general public, a new market.

My approach is simple: I use property management as a foundation for my ecosystem. I run four to five other companies under one roof and have control over all levels of service. With diversification and efficient use of my human and property resources, I can then secure bigger and beefier sales, more cleaning contracts, more lawn care contracts, more snow removal contracts, and more maintenance contracts. The whole process is the making of the Doorpreneur.

It's funny, because as my other businesses grew, I could feel increased respect for what I do. Many people don't recognize the power of property management on the entrepreneurial scale, but when they see new companies emerging from your core base, they understand your business formula is really working and is pretty impressive. I kept the pressure on myself, hunting for new business and opportunities that put me in the right places to get new contracts.

At my teaching and speaking engagements, people ask me how they can use a central business to generate profitable spin-off businesses. I consistently tell them it is all about planning. By properly planning what you want to do in business, you give yourself a head start. The second thing is to execute your plan with precision and a long-term strategic plan. And execution is nothing more than a series of rituals and routines that bring you to your goal.

I map out my rituals and routines for days, weeks, and months in a notebook that I carry with me at all times. And then, I set aside some pocket of time each day to work on execution because otherwise all I want to accomplish would remain on a piece of paper.

NEXT STEPS

Determine your entrepreneurial style. Are you a visionary, a master planner, a technician, or some combination of all of these things? Do you have the right people around you to complement your skills or have you fallen into the trap of working with people like you?

Gauge your vision. Does it stretch ahead far enough? How many businesses have you started in life? When do you come up with ideas and in what degree of detail before you get started? Do you think your vision tends to be too big or too small?

CHAPTER 4

IT'S TIME FOR PURPOSEFUL WORK

Why are you doing what you're doing? For most people, this is one of the hardest questions to answer. It's one that requires you to look deep within yourself to truly understand what drives you and why.

Adults employed full time in the US report working an average of 47 hours per week, which equates to nearly six days a week, according to a 2015 Gallup poll. That's a huge percentage of our lives. Shouldn't we be doing more than earning a paycheck? I sure do! I often laugh when I hear or see people overjoyed that it's Friday, when they can escape work. Don't get me wrong, I love my weekends just as much as the next person, but I've never had that gloom and doom feeling when I wake up and have to go to work. I consider myself quite fortunate that I've always loved what I've done.

My career as a software engineer was one of the most exciting times of my life. I was exposed to situations that made me grow as a person, both professionally and socially. I got to work with some of the largest companies in the world and some of the smartest people I've ever met. I also was able to travel the world, which gave me more of a global perspective. I loved what I did and I loved the people with whom I worked. It prepared me for becoming a Doorpreneur.

Figuring out one's purpose has become a popular pursuit among entrepreneurs today, and I see a lot of millennials pitching business ideas associated with a cause. It could be environmentally friendly products or donating a pair of socks for every pair purchased. All of these people are fueled by a purpose and it is this purpose that will propel them to success.

DIGGING DEEP

Before reading Cal Newport's book, *Deep Work: Rules for Focused Success in a Distracted World*, I had no real concept of "deep work," but instinctively, I kind of knew what it meant. I also was very aware of my need for space and time alone for my version of it. Without purpose in my work, I get bored and being bored can kill any business at any moment. I've seen guys burn entire businesses down in a flash because they lost interest; the businesses no longer fulfilled them. This is why it's so important to seek purpose. It will get you through those moments of doubt and boredom.

The property management world can be ruthless with your time, and if you're not careful, you'll see months go by with nothing being done "on" your business. If you have a company of a decent size, people come in and out of your office, and the phones ring all day. Making time to reflect and create, and find a more purposeful way to do things, is still necessary, however. If you make the time to get into deep work, you will very quickly realize if you are doing work with or without purpose. It will jump out at you in a flash!

The property management industry has a multitude of opportunities to find purpose. For our investors, real estate investments often represent their retirement. No pressure, right? For our tenants, we provide housing. Consider the many ways to add value and meaning to your day as a property manager. It could be by working with tenants with special needs. It could come from helping people enjoy their dream vacations as you manage second homes.

If you never take the time to slow down and ask yourself what this is all for, you may never find that ultimate purpose. If there is anything that keeps me up at night it is the thought of not living up to my true potential. I know I need to do something that makes a difference.

THREE GOALS

Despite clichés like "show me the money" in the movies and books urging you to follow the almighty dollar, successful businesses are never just about wealth accumulation. I always liked what Steve Jobs said, "I was worth about over $1 million when I was 23, and over $10 million when I was 24, and over $100 million when I was 25, and it wasn't that important. I never did it for the money."

From the time I made the decision to go into property management, I had three big goals. Initially, I wanted to build the biggest and best management company in my community. Within a short time, I expanded that goal to build the biggest and best firm in my field in the Maritime Provinces.

Next, I wanted to revolutionize the property management business, helping to raise its standards and generate the respect it deserved. Within a few years of my journey, I had started a management program called "pmology." The goal was to bring property management to a wider audience and begin to build a bank of shareable information about higher standards, better training, enhanced technology, and ways to create a better image for our industry. In fact, this book is an outcome of that initiative.

Third, I wanted to build a business empire from the foundation of a property management company. I saw the big picture of Doorpreneurship from the start. I understood that an industry that had to train the best landscapers, snow removal and maintenance people, cleaners, marketers, and sales personnel was in an ideal position to spin off into related businesses that could extend to a broader base of clients, including those who owned both commercial and residential businesses.

It took me a year to strategize and determine exactly *what* I wanted to build and months of planning to figure out *how* to build it. If you read carefully, you'll notice that not one of my goals said specifically that I wanted to get rich and fill my pockets, though obviously I needed to make money to sustain myself and those who depend on me. If you are eager to get your business growing or want to take your existing business to new levels, I encourage you to think bigger than your immediate goals of getting a few apartments to manage.

There are good reasons for this, and the best is that when you think big, you get your head out of the space of everything you have been told and move into an area where you can see things for yourself. Conversely, if you think small, you stay small. For example, most of us are raised to think that a good goal in life is to get as much education as possible and then try to find a secure job. I am a big proponent of education, but the numbers of letters after a person's name, however impressive, doesn't predict their ability to be successful in business.

As far as getting a job and focusing on keeping it, that doesn't work if you want to be an entrepreneur. Remember, if you spend your life working for others, you create wealth for them but you never really get a taste of it yourself. I think if Bill Gates had gone to school and gotten a steady job, he wouldn't be one of the richest men in the world today nor would he have enhanced the lives of millions of people.

Thinking big also prompts you to look at the lives of others who thought big and to see what they managed to accomplish. When you do that, the myths and misconceptions of what it takes to be successful start to fall away, and you see clearly that success is really within the grasp of everyone who wants it, plans for it, and works for it.

You don't have to come from a privileged background or have major political or business connections to start down the road of building a business empire. You don't have to live in a large, sophisticated urban center where millions of people can be tapped to be customers instead of a few thousand in your immediate geographic area. As long as you can think big, you can be big. You have to let go of the strings that tie you to your comfort zone and stretch yourself to look over the edge into a vast and interesting world.

That's when you start to see the things that you are passionate about and your enthusiasm kicks in. It triggers your creative spirit and leads you to ask, "What if?"

Finally, broadening your perspective allows you to see a purpose beyond merely trading your labor for wages to buy what you need to sustain yourself. Instead, you start to look at the impact your success could have on others, from your family and your community to your colleagues and ultimately, your industry.

MY FIRST LIFE-CHANGING MOMENT

Work has always been an essential component in my life, and I believe that outlook is important to me and to everyone who wants to find purpose in his or her life. My grandparents ran a convenience store when I was young, and I recall helping out in the store as early as 10 years old. I started with stocking shelves, doing odd jobs, and learning all about customer service.

Not long after, I took my first real paying job in a strip mall pet store in the north end of town. My mother managed the building, and they told her they needed someone to help clean the animal's cages and do other odd jobs. I was happy to do just about anything at that age as long as I could get some cold, hard cash in my hands. Looking back, my job was to make sure the animals had a comfortable place to live until they found homes. Kind of sounds familiar, right? (Life has a special way of unfolding. Try to be conscious of it.)

In high school, I started a four-year stint working in a restaurant. It was a bustling place, and I did just about every job they had. I started as a busboy and made my way into the kitchen. I turned into a really good steak guy. It was a fun place to work because about 10 to 15 of my friends also worked there.

That was another experience that helped develop my attitude about work and its purpose in my life. I saw that working with a great team of people in a friendly, respectful environment could be fun. It's not like we didn't have to work hard—we did. But we did it in such a way that it wasn't a burden. I looked forward to my shifts.

When I graduated high school, the university was not immediately in the cards for me, but I knew I had to support myself so I got a job at a call center. I made decent money and continued to live at home so it was all manageable for a couple of years. I learned some skills and secured two promotions. Again, work was my teacher as well as my means of sustenance. I discovered I had a strong intuitive sense of how to handle people and figure out solutions to their problems. I enjoyed doing that; it gave me a sense of satisfaction to help make people feel better.

I had no idea where all these work experiences would take me, but I was instinctively aware from the start that work was an essential component of my life and my personal development. I was still a teenager when I developed a work philosophy centered on purpose and was eager to see the big picture in everything I tackled. That awakening was likely what pushed me out of the call center environment. I started wondering where all those hours were taking me and I envisioned a different destination.

Change was only possible if I could achieve more education so I lined up a student loan and told my mother I was going back to school. She was both surprised and thrilled. I decided to follow my interest in computers and enroll in a one-year course focusing on network administration.

Unlike my early school years, and perhaps because I entered this course under my own steam, college was love at first sight and I couldn't stop studying. Everything made sense and it was easy for me. I was in an unprecedented flow and it was amazing. It led me to a 15-year career with Platform Computing, which was ultimately acquired by IBM.

Even though I was extremely intimidated by colleagues with PhDs in various computer-related fields, it pushed me to learn everything I could about the software I supported and the technologies around it. I was in love with the work that I was doing. To say I was passionate would be an understatement. I lived and breathed my work. Even though I started off in a lower ranking position, I always found purpose in what I was doing in order to better serve the company.

To go through each day totally disengaged with what you are spending hours doing makes no sense to me. It cannot help build you as a person, or inspire others around you, or move you closer to your goals. You and I both deserve much more than that in life.

Work is still noble because it moves our civilization as well as our economy. It needs to be honored in our society.

You can better support that philosophy if you see how every task leads you to a better place, a better job, a bigger business or a new opportunity as well as a means of sustaining yourself and those you love. Each time you complete a job, you become more capable and confident and find the courage apply those skills to other areas of your life. Understand and have the faith to accept that when you start something, it will take you somewhere else if you open your mind and teach yourself to think of a bigger picture.

FINDING YOUR MENLO PARK

Someone who has inspired me greatly is Thomas Edison. Most people know him for his big inventions like the light bulb and the phonograph, but I know him for his amazing work ethic and dedication. Few people know that he released at least one minor invention every week—and a major one every month.

When I was at IBM, my interest in Edison and his work methods intensified. I was doing a lot of work at the time with General Electric (GE), one of our clients, and I still remember the emotion I felt when I first entered one of the GE facilities and saw Edison's desk right in the front lobby. It was sealed off, not to be touched.

I was taken by it, not for its novelty but for what it represented. I have no doubt that he was sitting at this desk when he came up with some of his biggest ideas. As the money from his inventions started to make his bank balance healthier, he built his Menlo Park Laboratory, which was considered state-of-the-art in its day and one of the best labs in the world. (The desk I saw actually had been at Menlo Park.)

Edison created this space so he could do his best work. His unique body rhythm pushed him to work all night and then sleep until noon; it was just the way he was wired. By having an ideal workplace, he was able to be productive and innovative for years.

Standing there looking at his desk, I began to wonder then, as I do today, where is *my* Menlo Park? I think we all need to find the space where we do our best work, where our mind is able to expand and imagine, and where our ideas can be recognized, captured, and analyzed, then acted upon quickly and effectively.

My office is full of disruptions and interruptions. To ensure that I continue to evolve as a dreamer and that I don't get stuck as a doer of endless repeated tasks, I have to remove myself from the traditional work environment and go to my home office. That's where I can get quiet time to reflect and plan to reach my next stage as a Doorpreneur.

We all need to be relaxed when we do our best work. We need to be able to think out a concept fully before our train of thought is hijacked by someone else's emergency. I suspect this is why our industry has not advanced as it should. If you work in an environment where you spend every minute handling daily fires and activities, you won't have time to innovate.

Edison was a master innovator. He had the gift of vision and the ability to keep many ideas and projects progressing on the front and back burners of his brain. He was adept at moving his ideas from concept to reality, something that's challenging for most of us.

Enter property management today. The time is here for similar innovation in this industry. With the advent of new technology, we can effect major change if we adapt it to work for our bigger purposes. Property management is essentially a systems-based business and it's possible to automate many of the tasks that consume us daily.

It's up to us to find new ways to make our management systems more efficient so that we have time to reflect and apply our creativity and new ideas to related businesses as we build our empire.

NEXT STEPS

Locate your Menlo Park. Where do you do your deepest, most innovative work? If you don't have this space, where could you create it and how quickly can you accomplish this?

Find the time. What routines can you develop to simplify your business so you have time to think, analyze, and create? Are you working *in* your business or *on* your business? If you want to build an empire from your property management foundation, you must find the time and quiet space to work on it.

CHAPTER 5

HOW DO I BECOME A DOORPRENEUR?

The road to becoming a Doorpreneur starts with the property management business. You will hear me come back to this a lot because it's without a doubt the most important piece of the Doorpreneurship puzzle. Without creating a solid foundation, nothing else can be built.

It took me several years before I thought of adding on to the management company. We were so busy building the business that we had zero time to even think about anything else. This is the way it should be. You want a thriving management company and being so busy is a great sign that you're doing something right.

What defines a successful management company? This is a somewhat subjective question, but this is what I think it should look like:

1. There should be a clear leader and a solid strategy for where to take the company. Whether you are by yourself or you have a team of employees, you need to have someone at the helm steering the ship and that person needs to know where they are going.

2. The company should be profitable! This means that there are healthy profits left for the ownership team after everyone is paid. The exact profit margins are not set in stone; however, as a company, we always strive to hit a minimum of 20 percent. If you have not been able to demonstrate solid returns on the management piece, starting something else is simply going to make things worse. The new venture will distract you and you'll risk blowing it all up. Creating a new company is something anyone can do. Creating a *profitable* company is what separates success from failure.

3. Your staff is happy and love what they do. I will be the first to admit that I've not always been the best boss, and I'm not the strongest person when it comes to dealing with personnel matters. This is where my partner comes in. He's very good in these situations, and that's one of the reasons why we make a great team. Given the stress of day-to-day operations, you have to be proactive with your staff to ensure that they don't get burned out.

4. Your operations must be on point. In the world of property management, that means that the systems and processes are implemented and followed by all.

5. Marketing and sales are key drivers for the company. In short, this means that the company is able to produce quality leads and able to close them. Without a stream of new business coming in, a management company can and will struggle.

Based on my experience, transitioning from property manager to Doorpreneur requires two distinct mindsets: The entrepreneur (visionary) and the technician. The entrepreneur needs to be able to see what is possible, and the technician has to have the ability to take that dream and turn it into reality. These, along with a number of other skills, are required to fully prepare for the world of Doorpreneurship.

Most property management companies are owner-operated; however, we're starting to see larger management companies that need a lot more help to run the company. As a Doorpreneur, you can't do it all alone. It would be very difficult for any one person to continue running a successful management company while starting new secondary brands. Thinking back to when I started my management company, I knew within a month of starting that I needed a technician to help me. I urge you to consider the same.

Operating a property management business is unique, but there is no better business to gain insight into all the businesses that evolve from it and to develop your expertise. Let's go through some high-level challenges that are crucial for you to keep in mind as you consider becoming a Doorpreneur.

As property managers, we typically control all the money. It's really a beautiful thing. We collect rents, pay bills, and pay ourselves. Every month, our management fees are paid to our operating account. It's never late. I never have to make a call, and I never have to deal with nonpayment. I didn't really appreciate this until we ventured outside of our little bubble and offered our first service to the general public.

Once you venture outside the safe haven of your management business, you will need to keep a very close eye on your accounts payable and receivable. This is especially true if you provide a service that offers clients various payment terms.

As soon as you give your clients a certain amount of time to pay your invoices, you need to remember that your bills and payroll still have to be paid within certain existing timeframes that may not coincide with when you get paid! This is when you will be faced with cash flow issues. To properly deal with cash flow crunches, a good strategy is to have a slush fund with several months of operating cash in case of emergency. Another strategy is to have an open line of credit to dip into when needed.

Staffing is another challenging area. It goes without saying that if you're going to go big, you'll need a lot of people to help you along the way. A management company still can stay pretty lean, depending on how it decides to run operations. I've seen management companies take care of more than 500 units with four staff members. I've also seen companies with the same number of units employ more than 10 employees.

The difference comes down to the services you provide. A company with only four employees will typically sub everything out. Property management has a lot of backend administration processes that need to be done on a weekly/monthly basis. This is perfect work for virtual assistants, and management companies are taking advantage of this lower cost workforce to handle noncritical administrative tasks.

In contrast, a company with more than 10 employees is most likely doing everything in-house. Nothing is subbed out. They do all the property management, leasing, accounting, maintenance, and cleaning, and proper staffing is required. Both of these methods work and can provide their owners with good financial results. Personally, after watching my mother run her business, I've always opted to keep as much as I could in-house. I liked that she was able to control a lot of the stuff thrown at her. Her company also seemed to make more money with this model.

This doesn't mean that you can't make money using subs. Just about any company in any industry marks up work that they sub out because there's a lot of work that goes into hiring and managing them.

A good question to ask is, "Do I want to have a lot of staff or not?" If you like the smaller, lean model, be careful how you add onto your business. Most new ventures will require you to have additional staff under your watch. I've always dreamed of having a big business that employed lots of people and providing a workplace for others to grow and provide for their families has been one of my greatest accomplishments.

Money and capital is another critical area—more specifically, the cash needed to be invested into a new venture. As property managers, we are incredibly fortunate that we can start a management company with very little funding, but the reality of most businesses is that you need some cash up front.

If you do things right, you should rarely need to inject cash into the business unless you're investing in some new software, opening a new location, or maybe looking to hire a new staff member who may take some time to produce income. When we got into the landscaping and snow removal business, we were faced with some very big investments just to get started. It all worked out in the end, but you need to be financially prepared to take advantage of opportunities as you see them.

Sir Richard Branson, a serial entrepreneur who has always inspired me with his ventures into air travel, space travel, hotel development, and even cruise lines, believes that starting your own business isn't just a job. "It's a way of life," he said.

Of course, he also said that if you are embarking around the world in a hot air balloon, you shouldn't forget the toilet paper, so he is obviously a planner as well as a person who enjoys building businesses.

And that is precisely what you have been doing since you started this book. You have been considering where you could take a property management business. You are looking at how to tap into a larger marketplace and gain access to more customers. And now you're probably wondering how to start off as a Doorpreneur.

GROWING BEYOND YOUR RENT ROLL

Going down the Doorpreneur road means that you're looking to grow beyond your rent roll and take all that you've learned from the management company and apply it to another business. In my opinion, the easiest way to get started is with services that every management company needs: property maintenance and cleaning.

There are a number of other options that also are natural spin-offs. These include trash and recycling, accounting services, tenant finding and screening, appliance repair, and call centers that handle property showings and afterhours inquiries to name a few.

You might be wondering whether you are a Doorpreneur if you already do all of your in-house maintenance and cleaning. My answer is that you're halfway there! The true sign of Doorpreneurship is offering your product or service to the general public. That's where the real magic happens.

For the purpose of this book and from my own experience, we will use maintenance as the first service that can be used as a launchpad to Doorpreneurship. There are typically two ways to run maintenance within a management firm. You either hire your own staff or you sub it out to third party contractors. Either one can work. From a Doorpreneur perspective, doing the work in-house is the more obvious choice.

The financial model for a maintenance business is pretty straightforward. You devise an hourly rate for your various services and charge accordingly. As you figure out your hourly rate, be sure to incorporate items like insurance, workers' compensation, benefits, vacations, vehicles, and fuel. All of those things add up quickly. You are running a business, not a charity, so you have to be sure you cover your costs and still make a profit.

Make sure your margins are such that you are profitable *and* your clients are still getting great service at a good price. You are not there to compete with the guys who charge $15 per hour cash. You will never win in that space. If a property owner insists on doing some of the work themselves or on using their "own" people, you need to decide if you want to work with them or not. Sometimes it works out well; other times, it's a disaster. My rule of thumb is that we do it all or we don't do business.

MAINTENANCE IS THE BACKBONE OF YOUR BUSINESS

As a property manager, you learn quickly that a good maintenance team is vital because maintenance is typically the number one issue with most tenants. It has to be a priority in property management because handling it well is a must if you intend to grow your brand.

At one point, I employed seven full-time maintenance workers in just one of our locations. I quickly recognized that maintenance really was a separate business with very different logistics.

Property maintenance (within the management company) is a service in which you have not one but two clients. One is the property owner and the other is the tenant. Whether you do your maintenance in-house or you sub it out, your management staff must stay on top of the work orders.

One of the first things I wish I had done earlier on is to have created some sort of master list of regular maintenance issues and the time needed to fix them. Painting is the most common service, and it's a good idea to know how long it should take to paint your units. A good way to do this is to have your best painter and your slowest painter paint an apartment and then compare the times. Apartment conditions will vary; however, this exercise gives you a good baseline.

The maintenance staff for your management company can be divided into two categories: Runners and turnovers. At least, that's what we call them. The runner is the maintenance person who is on call for a particular week since we need to be available 24/7. Every week, we rotate on-call duties among the maintenance staff. Without a doubt, this is one of the toughest parts of the job for the staff. Some weeks can be a breeze and others can be a flurry of nonstop calls, day and night.

The runner's calls typically consist of small, urgent tasks and, if time allows, nonurgent jobs. These jobs are usually done in units that are occupied so some coordination with tenants is required.

The turnover position has a different role. Every month, property managers deal with turnovers in units. As one tenant leaves and another prepares to move in, everything must be ready for the new tenants. The maintenance work to be done in the units can be small, simple fixes, or complete paint jobs, or even completely gutting and renovating a bathroom. As you've learned by now, anything can happen!

You need to be ready to handle your turnovers. We've found it helpful to do prechecks on all outgoing units a week or two before the tenant moves out. This gives us a good idea of what to expect by the first of the month. Being on top of scheduling is of critical importance in this stage. Our jobs are to turn over units as quickly and as efficiently as possible so our owners don't lose any income.

If your property management company is not big enough to have both runners and turnover staff, outsource painting since it is pretty easy to find good painters. Keep your good carpenters busy with the other work.

Technology also plays a huge role in maintenance because you need a system to track your work orders. Most property management software providers have maintenance modules. We currently use Buildium for our work order management and it works well for us.

THE "WOW" FACTOR

When you open your business doors to the general public, you'll be exposed to a lot of things quickly. You are no longer your own client—you have to report to others. Your standards, professionalism, work, and reputation must be on point. In my opinion, this is where good property managers can become great Doorpreneurs. If you've done things properly, you should be able to start serving your new client base with ease.

It's worth noting that I ran the maintenance division under the same umbrella as my property management company for many years. But when we offered these maintenance services to the public, it became apparent I needed to carve it into a new brand. Internally, we didn't have to worry about things like sales or marketing. This changed once we started serving the general public, and we needed a new brand to be able to properly articulate our message. We didn't want to get it confused with our management business.

Always be conscious that providing services to the public requires you to play at a different level. Your quotes must be tight, margins must be understood, and most of all, the experience must deliver a "wow" factor to the customer.

You also might have to implement things like a fleet of vehicles, uniforms, and publicity materials. Remember that the handyman market in any community is full of fly-by-night players who are not always known for their skill or scruples. If you do it right, this is your opportunity to shine, and recommendations spread like wildfire. Be ready for your maintenance business to take off on its own!

THE CLEANING SERVICE MODEL

I always knew maintenance could be split off into a separate business with a broader client base. I also recognized cleaning had the same potential. I learned from my mother it was best to have cleaning done with in-house staff for the same reasons that it was best to use in-house maintenance. I hired my first full-time cleaner and my second maintenance person after I had 100 units.

Just as with maintenance, hiring great cleaning people is important. When you have just rented a property and your new prospects want to move in as soon as possible, you need staff whom you can count on to make the extra effort. With great staff, you can move mountains.

Like maintenance, cleaning also has two distinct functions: Turnover cleaning and regular common area cleaning. We nearly always need to send cleaners to work on turnovers. In addition, if you manage larger apartment buildings or commercial buildings, there's a lot of regular cleaning to do in the common areas of the building. Those include areas like the hallways, the entrances, additional amenities such as a gym, pool and social rooms, and elevators. My staff works primarily in either one division or the other (turnovers or regular duties).

The fees associated with cleaning are almost identical to the maintenance world. When you're ready to create a separate cleaning firm that taps into the general public market, I suggest new construction and commercial properties as places that offer great opportunities.

New construction cleaning is a great way to start. We started by working with local builders to clean newly built apartment buildings. This tends to work out very well because, as a property manager, you already have all the knowledge of how to properly clean individual units and building common areas. Working with the developer also provides a great way to parlay your skills into other opportunities such as management for the property or to become their go-to for construction cleanup jobs.

Another avenue for securing clients is commercial cleaning. Most, if not all, commercial properties have professional cleaners looking after the common areas and individual spaces within the building. Warehouses are another great place to seek cleaning opportunities.

NEXT STEPS

Research your pricing model. Check your area to determine fees for painting, plumbing, electrical, carpentry, and flooring work, and start to create a pricing model that will work as you prepare to establish a separate maintenance company.

Train staff to deal with the public. Make sure to provide your maintenance staff with some additional skills in communications and customer relations. You may be able to outsource this training if you lack the corporate resources to handle it.

CHAPTER 6

THE ART AND SCIENCE OF PROPERTY MANAGEMENT

"I can't believe I ever got into this business! What was I thinking?" These were the exact words of a friend of mine who decided to start a third-party management company. The truth is, I wasn't sure if he was going to succeed. I knew that he had a lot going for him as well as a lot going against him.

He was a very successful real estate agent in addition to personally owning several hundred doors. Being a landlord was not new to him. He was starting to get more and more involved in the world of buying and selling apartments, and he figured it would be easy to offer an extension of his internal management services to outside clients (mostly clients from his sales side).

This is how a lot of property managers get into the business. They either own properties themselves and cannot find other good managers or they see it as a new growth opportunity. Either way, they are coming into the game with some experience. You would think that their backgrounds would guarantee success and transform them into superstars, right? Wrong. Over the years, I've seen both sides: I've seen people make an amazing transition, and I've seen people completely fall flat on their faces.

My friend told me that landing new clients was exciting, but dealing with all of the other issues that come with management was too much. He had a lot of low-end properties and discovered that taking care of his own properties was much different than caring for others.

Like it or not, if you decide to make a career in the third-party property management business and you own most of your portfolio, conflicts of interest are inevitable. This is why I made the decision early on to own very few properties so I would not favor them. Let's be honest, it would be very easy to do just that.

Another challenge is that not everyone takes care of their properties in the same way. I've worked with many investors and they all have their own way of doing things. Taking the time to know how to please them all is not easy—nor is it for everyone, including my friend.

"The amount of work and headache that is needed to manage these properties is not financially worth it," he said. "I can make more money selling one building than I can make managing a property for five years!"

FACING THE ULTIMATE CHALLENGE

Unfortunately, his statement is accurate. An agent can broker a deal for a one million dollar apartment building and make $50K in commission versus earning $7,200 a year in property management fees. It would take almost seven years of management to match the realtor's commission rate.

Yes, you're reading that right. Almost seven years! Crazy, right?

This is why it's very hard for real estate agents to make a good run in property management. The income versus workload is imbalanced. After calling it quits in just over a year, my friend sold off all his management contracts and continued taking care of his own properties. To this day, he still refers a lot of his clients to property managers like us. He is still very much in the mindset that third-party management is not for him, but it could have been if he had done it right.

This chapter is going to teach you the concepts behind the art and science of property management that would have helped my friend. I have no doubt about that. No matter where you are in your entrepreneurial journey, you'll find this information impactful. Internalize it, study it, and put it into action, and you'll reap the rewards.

THE ART OF PROPERTY MANAGEMENT

Do you live by any kind of code? I do.

I'm not a military guy, but I am someone who appreciates structure and living by certain rules. Many property managers let their days run them as opposed to running their days. It's not wrong; it just makes things much more painful than they really have to be. There is undeniable raw power in being able to design, control, and execute your day according to *your* plan.

So many of you see the property management industry as a single service platform: You manage properties. This is not a bad way of seeing things. I'll go even further and say that it can be amazing if it's what you are looking for. Your life, your business, and your lifestyle can be great with just this simple recipe. I've seen people attain tremendous success managing just 100 doors, so it's possible.

It's not my nature to stop there so I always have to ask, "What if I could be more?" We all have this part of us that asks, what if? It is that part of us that dreams up new ideas and gets goosebumps just thinking about them. What if you could tap into your preexisting zone of genius and expand it?

You might have gotten into the business on purpose, or you could be like most property managers who fell into it by accident and then decided to go deeper. Either way, if you've made it past one-and-a-half years in the business, there's a good chance you'll be around for a while and the industry has not eaten you alive.

DEVELOPING THE PROPERTY MANAGER'S CODE

Over the years, I've seen a lot. I turned 43 in 2019, and I've been in the industry my entire life. I've had the opportunity to watch my mother, the most amazing person I know, teach me about property management. She defined to me what it means to care for others, and that is the cornerstone of what this business is all about.

As a result, I've been able to distill my years of learning the business into what I believe are the foundational tools required to succeed in property management, and it all starts with a code.

This code defines how we go about our day-to-day activities and how we see and treat the world around us. There are three tenets to my code:

- Lead with a servant's heart.

- Practice "get it done" leadership.
- Maintain a simplicity mindset.

LEAD WITH A SERVANT'S HEART

What does it mean to be a leader? What does it mean to serve?

It means that you adhere to three key behaviors and by exhibiting them yourself, you build them into the culture of your business. They are:

- Treat people with respect.
- Serve before reward.
- People before profits.

These three tenets have the power to transform a company if you truly allow them. If you look at 100 thriving property management companies, you will without doubt find a handful of leaders who practice the art of servant leadership, even if they don't know it.

I've seen servant leadership in action, and it's a beautiful thing to behold. It's second nature for some people while it may require a concentrated effort by others. Regardless, the day you decide to put people before profits is the day you decide to transform your business.

As a property manager, you typically encounter three to five different groups of people every day: Owners, tenants, staff members, vendors, and new prospects. Our entire world revolves around people and relationships, and our conversations are not always easy or fun. We often deal with serious topics, and our relationships tend to be long term so we can't be shortsighted.

Serving our clients is at the heart of what we do and who we are as property managers. We go out of our way to make a tenant's day and let our owners feel like they have the best staff taking care of their properties.

PRACTICE "GET IT DONE" LEADERSHIP

"Get it done" leadership involves getting the work done in a manner that involves every member of our team taking responsibility for their actions.

Every day we must walk into the office expecting the unexpected, and every day we're put into situations where we must make some difficult choices. That is the nature of what we do. You have to be prepared to handle whatever comes up and be willing to do yourself what you ask of others. In the world of property management, this style of leadership is required to succeed.

My business partner has been by my side for more than 10 years, and we've gone through just about every scenario imaginable. We are both willing to go out and do just about anything we ask our staff to do, and we employ an amazing team of people who live by the same code. When you lead by example and do what it takes to get a job done, you create an atmosphere of care and respect that is felt by everyone. That's important considering the sensitivity required to deal with people and their homes.

The foundations of "get it done" leadership are action and accountability. By accountability, I mean the obligation to accept responsibility for one's actions. It's a scary word, especially in property management, when so many things can go wrong at any time of the day or night.

Taking full responsibility for something can be intimidating, and I get it, but it's necessary if you want to be great in this industry. And by "great," I mean world class.

My inspiration on accountability comes from an amazing book called *The Leader Who Had No Title* by Robin Sharma, who argues that anyone can be a leader. Robin shares the story of a man who cleaned the bathrooms at Johannesburg Airport in South Africa. He greeted everyone who entered by saying, "Welcome to my office." His "office" was spotless, and he took great pride in his work. That sense of accountability and pride is the magic that separates an average worker from a great one.

That's the type of attitude you want in your office. That's the type of person with whom your owners, tenants, and vendors want to deal. These are the types of colleagues with whom your top players want to work! Hold yourself accountable, take full ownership of what you do, and expect the same from others.

A SIMPLICITY MINDSET

As humans, we are very good at making things complicated when they don't need to be. In most situations, simple instructions and basic communication can solve the toughest of problems. Want to make your business more predictable and sustainable?

Simplify everything!

The complications of property management can be downright crippling but only if you let them. Over the past 10 years, I've had my share of ups and downs with my management firm. Sometimes I got so overwhelmed that I froze, unable to do anything.

Why? The short answer is that I lacked systems and tended to complicate things, even though property management is a fairly predictable business. Every month, we go through the same cycles; therefore, reliable and documented systems should be in place, especially as the business grows.

A perfect example for this is with our monthly inspections when tenants move in and out of units. For each procedure, someone from my company must be present to complete a conditions report of the apartment by filling out a simple checklist. They don't have to worry about what to include or what not to include. They just follow the list.

Completing the report is just one part of a long process, but having a standard checklist makes things much easier for those who have to do the work and for those who have to look over the work being done.

By creating a process chain, linking it with checklists and checkpoints, you create an environment that has clarity. That clarity will show up in every aspect of your business, including your bank account!

THE SCIENCE OF PROPERTY MANAGEMENT

The scientific part of property management involves how you create and use systems to operate your business in addition to some key strategies for building and cultivating relationships. If you've been in the industry for some time, you'll know that everything we do is typically tracked in some sort of checklist.

More than almost any other business, property management falls into a recurring series of predictable cycles, and this is how we build predictable and sustainable practices. Once you chart these cycles, you are in a better position to devise ways to handle them more efficiently. They include rent collection, moves in and out, evictions, applications, maintenance, on-boarding owners, on-boarding tenants, and leasing agreements signed and then renewed.

All businesses, especially property management, have interrelated processes and they need to be written down. Take the time to explain to your staff the purpose and motivation for each task. Your documentation process should reflect how you conduct business.

When that is accomplished, certain patterns and places where processes overlap can be seen. Improvements and fine tuning can happen only after these essential steps are documented. Pilots don't take off without going through their checklist and they hold the safety of hundreds of passengers in their hands. So why would you want to manage property without creating your own lists? There is no industry standard when it comes to a common set of operating procedures or lists, but here are a few lists that we use in our business.

The first is our Move-in Inspection list. This is a critical document that in essence describes the condition of a unit when a tenant moves in and is helpful in case of damages during their tenancy. I've seen some lists that are one page long and others that are five pages. It really comes down to personal preference as well as the city regulations that govern your business.

Our second most popular list is the Vacancy list. This is our bible. When you have more than 1,000 units in one location, you need to be on top of your vacancies. Every morning, we start our day with a

Team Huddle where we go over the day's priorities but also review and update our vacancy list. Every day in a larger management office, units are rented and tenants give notice. It's typical.

We need to make sure that everything is up to date on this list because it affects other things. As an example, as soon as a unit is rented, we have to start by removing any current ads, which can include lawn signs as well as ads online. The circumstances are reversed when a current tenant gives us notice that they intend to move.

By studying your lists, not only can you spot obvious flaws but you also can see ways that certain tasks can be combined to reduce time. You may decide to decrease resources needed for certain jobs and find ways to enhance quality. You also can minimize unnecessary movement between departments and guard against task duplication.

Ultimately, look for ways you can hike customer and employee satisfaction. The more you can fine tune these cycles, establish efficient processes, and manage your rent roll, the better.

STRATEGIC RELATIONSHIPS

I've said it once and I'll say it again: Property management is all about relationships. When I first started my management company, I knew that some key relationships would be the difference that would separate me from everyone else. In particular, I recognized that creating and cultivating partnerships with realtors would provide me with a great source of leads.

When I started my management company, I was not a licensed realtor, and I think that helped me tremendously because I did not present a threat. If you're in the real estate sales world, you know how ruthless it can be. The last thing a realtor wants to do is refer a client your way if they fear you'll steal them away.

If you are a licensed realtor (as I am now), you must find ways around this. I operate on the 80/20 rule: I focus my time and energy on the 20 percent of agents who are busy and generate 80 percent of the sales. Depending on the type of properties with which you work, your prospective list may be as small as a handful of agents. I work with two to three, though I get calls once in a while from others. We've created a system that works beautifully for us.

Once you have your group, you need to constantly nurture those relationships. That can take the form of regular check-ins via email or going out for lunch or even for a drink or two. Your most important job is to make sure you are always at the top of their minds when it comes to rentals or new management.

It's also your job to keep an eye out for opportunities where you can help them. I've always been very generous with listings, especially when I lacked marketing experience. Giving realtors a listing is one of the most powerful gestures you can make to reciprocate their generosity with you.

Another great strategy that has made a world of difference throughout my career is getting to know as many real estate *investors* as possible. It's your job to know who owns what in your city. That's Property Management 101. I've lost count of the amount of times that I've stopped on the side of the road to write down the address of a building so I could look up who owned it when I got home.

Once I found a name, I would do whatever I needed to do to find out more about the owner. If they were local, did they own anything else?

Who managed the property? And, whom did I know who knew them? This all took time and commitment but definitely helped me in the long run. I've come to know just about every building and building owner in my city.

Once you get the owner's contact information, you need to get in front of them. My most successful strategy is to try and get a warm introduction through one of my contacts. Chances are very good that there is someone who knows the owner, and I'll ask for an introduction of some sort via email, or LinkedIn, or another social platform. From there, it's all up to me. Personally, I've never been one to try and sell someone on the first meeting. I like to build a relationship over time and then, when the opportunity arises, I will make the ask. Your job in this case is to make sure that you are seen as the expert and authority in property management in your area. That's the key, along with just being a good person.

In order to be seen as an authority and expert in your industry, you must be able to do a few different things. Your first task is to educate. Distribute content that educates people on what it is you do. This can be via email newsletters, social media, or "lunch & learns." Doing presentations at real estate brokerages in your city can be a great starting point for you to share your story and allow them to see who you really are.

Second, I urge you to become one with the written word. This can be as simple as starting a blog on your website or using social media. Writing is a powerful medium to share your thoughts and systems, and you'll stand out from the crowd if you do it well.

NEXT STEPS

Take stock of your internal systems. Don't make this more complicated than it needs to be. If you've owned and run the company for some time, you know where you're strong and where you're weak. Write it down and talk to your team about it.

Get involved in a property management group. This can be NARPM (North American Residential Property Managers) or any other local or online industry group. Ask questions, and find out what systems and processes have helped others.

CHAPTER 7

VALUE IS THE KEY

Property managers have the ultimate edge but most don't even see it.

What other business gives you the opportunity to work with clients for five, 10, and even 20 years? As you know, we have two clients—investors and tenants. For our investors, we are in charge of what could be their retirement fund so we will get their attention just about any time we want. That's what I call a superpower. Very rarely will one of my clients not immediately take my call. I often have to start my conversations by saying that everything is okay so they don't think I'm calling with bad news.

For our tenants, we provide them with a home. They may jump from one property to another, but many of them will stay with you for a long time if you treat them right. They like you, and, most important, they trust you to provide them with a safe and well-maintained residence. Your value is that you build relationships based on honesty, trust, loyalty, and those things govern every decision you make.

Many types of people will end up using your management services and living in your properties; it's up to you to know them well and to take every opportunity to serve them. By knowing their wants and needs, you can design your communication strategies in ways that are meaningful to them.

CREATING RELATIONSHIPS

The most important part of property management is not fixing toilets or cleaning hallways. It's about cultivating loyalty when you are fully engaged in doing things that matter most to building owners, tenants, and employees. At the end of the day, it's pretty simple: people will forget what you said, people will forget what you did, but people will never forget how you made them feel.

In the business of property management, the secret to success is ensuring that tenants are so happy they never want to leave. When you can substantially decrease tenant turnover, you can begin to really create wealth for your property owners. Otherwise, every time somebody moves out, it costs money in maintenance, cleaning, advertising, showing the property, securing the lease, handling the inspections, and getting new tenants moved in.

While there are exceptions to every situation, generally if you keep buildings clean and well-maintained, if you are responsive to calls for maintenance and assistance, and if you learn how to secure the right tenant base from the outset, you can dramatically impact tenant retention in your properties. You can enhance the feeling of attachment tenants have to their homes by building strong relationships with them.

From the earliest days when I saw my mother in property management, I saw the relationships she fostered were what mattered most. I remember how people loved her and how she remembered their names and details about their lives with great respect that was reciprocated. She had a "magic touch" I never forgot, even though I knew her job in our building was not always fun or easy. She was always respectful, and she never lost her cool. I learned from the best.

Today, I make an effort to remember the name of every tenant I meet, and you'll still find me visiting apartments and keeping those relationships alive. I remember details about their lives and the things that matter to them, sending them welcome packages and other gifts to acknowledge major milestones in their lives.

Building these relationships has always been important in property management, but the degree of importance has been amplified since the era of social media and the "sharing economy." Happy customers give great testimonials and reviews, and word-of-mouth endorsements are worth more than any marketing you can buy. In fact, personal recommendations have never been more critical.

A 2012 study conducted on behalf of Reward Stream, a provider of viral marketing, found that personal recommendations are the number one driver of consumer decisions at every stage of the business cycle, across multiple product categories. When it comes to spending money, 80 percent of the time purchases (regardless of price point) were most influenced by the recommendations of family and friends, researchers found.

This always surprises people given our digital age, but the bottom line in most cities is that if a friend or family member has a good experience living in an apartment building, they are more inclined to influence a friend or family member to follow their lead.

Ed Keller, whose firm conducted the study and who wrote *The Face-to-Face Book: Why Real Relationships Rule in a Digital Marketplace*, says the pivotal importance of recommendations should be comforting for entrepreneurs who have close personal connections with their customers. When you have happy tenants in your property management business and happy customers in your additional businesses, be sure to ask them if they would kindly recommend you to their family and friends. You'll be amazed by their positive responses. And if one of their recommendations works out, be sure to thank them.

VALUABLE LIFE LESSONS FROM DUBAI

In early 2015, I was contacted by a couple living in Dubai. They planned to relocate to Eastern Canada later that year and wanted some help finding a new home. I responded to their email right away, and we stayed in contact over the next few months. Immigrating to Canada was a big undertaking for them, and I felt the need to help them once they arrived.

After they called me to see what I had available, we narrowed down some prospective homes and started to book showings. Because they didn't have a vehicle, I picked them up and drove them to many of our appointments so we got to know each other quite well over the course of two weeks. We also happened to have a lot in common in terms of past careers and similar interests.

Since they were new immigrants to Canada, I also helped them arrange a lot of details for their children's school as well as simple things like registering for driver's licenses. During one of our visits, they told me they had reached out to several real estate agents in town to get information on other rental properties. Every agent they spoke to told them to call Ground Floor and talk to Tony. It was definitely a good sign that others respected and recommended my business.

They finally found the right property and we signed a year-long lease. It was a brand new house, which was perfect because they were concerned about maintenance challenges. They also loved the fact that it was modern. And I loved the fact that they were taking on a unit that someone else had backed out of at the last minute, leaving me with zero income. Had I dismissed these people when they first contacted me because their needs were not immediate, I never would have gotten that lease signed.

When you do the right thing and serve people honorably, it builds the goodwill and positive karma that keeps your business on track.

TREAT YOUR VENDORS LIKE GOLD

While I now have a staff of more than 50 employees, there are still times when I have to reach out to secure additional contractors. No staff member or contractor has ever had to chase me for money. They do the job for me, and they get paid and get paid quickly. I am loyal to them, and in turn, they are loyal to me.

Third party trades are critical to property managers, and when we need them, it's often due to an emergency. When you are a plumber, for example, and you get a middle-of-the-night call about a plugged-up toilet, you are a lot more apt to get out of bed and deal with it without complaints if you know you will be paid promptly. In fact, when you pay people on time, they end up putting your requests at the top of their list.

This is how trust and loyalty come into play in my businesses. In working with both staff and tenants, I have never subscribed to the "it's not personal, it's just business" theory. All business is personal. You don't need to insert yourself into everyone's personal lives, but you do need to be available when they need you.

BE RESPONSIVE

If you want to succeed as a Doorpreneur, this is one of the best pieces of advice I can give you: pick up your phone.

Sounds simple, right? You'd be surprised at how many people avoid this very small act. Don't shuffle people through a series of automated operators who take them anywhere but where they want to go. Say "hello," find out what they want, and assign it to be handled. Hire a great administrator so every call to your place of business gets a friendly and helpful response.

Also, be sure that neither you nor any member of your staff ever responds to a question with these awful words, "I don't know. That's not my job."

Everyone in my companies knows that's a phrase I never want to hear. When you're the client, you think it means, "I really don't give a sh--! I'm not going to help you."

If you honestly don't know the answer, it's okay to say, "I don't have the answer, but I will find it." Just don't leave anyone in limbo. You can say something like this, "Let me do some research for you and I will call you back with either the answer or with a status update by

5:00 p.m. today. Is that okay?" Then make sure you call them with the answer!

DEMAND EXCELLENCE

I've always wanted to achieve the same great reputation as my mother. To do that, I had to surround myself with people who had the same set of values as myself. You need to find people who are not just skilled workers but who also are fine human beings. That's what gives you the real edge.

If you drive up to one of your properties in a beat-up truck hauling a trailer full of junk or if you hire people who will accept only cash for their labor, you will find yourself with the worst of buildings and the most difficult of tenants. Property management as an industry is very unforgiving. If you get pegged as a certain style of manager, it is very hard to change that reputation. If you insist on quality from your staff and in the way you conduct your business, then you'll get quality properties to manage and decent tenants to live there.

To reduce stress, you also need quality clients who share your values. Forgetting this and accepting anyone as a client in your desperation to get business is a mistake. This resonates with me because we've been burned a couple of times by working with the wrong owners in our eagerness to add doors. Take the time to know what people are really about and vet them before you sign contracts.

I learned this the hard way a few years ago when we took over a beautiful new condo complex by the water. I saw red flags when they asked us to make a major change in our standard management agreement involving a clause on liability. I should have stayed true to my instincts, questioned them more, and done additional research, but I was eager to grow our business and agreed to manage the property. It was a terrible experience, and we soon discovered the property had major structural issues, and the condo board was trying to build a case to sue the developer.

I began to suspect that the condo board wanted to pass on liability to us because the building was defective, and we ended up in litigation. It was a lesson learned, and I'm thankful that we had good insurance. At the end of the day, we added a basic rule to our business: Never make changes to standard management contracts without consulting a lawyer.

Our management business works mostly with real estate investors and they are all different. Some have small portfolios and others have large ones. Some are micromanagers and some don't like to be bothered unless their building is on fire. It's our responsibility to recognize the types of owners with whom we want to work and who will enhance our business.

Specifically, our business model looks for owners who are growth oriented and who, like us, understand the value of good tenants and great service. They also need to understand the costs involved in renovating apartments and not try to cut every penny in half. And they need to be respectful to others and not get involved in every little detail.

Knowing this—and sticking to it—has made all the difference for us. Without anything else out there to guide us, we even developed our own "Ground Floor Starter Kit" to help us better assess potential owners. Remember your business relationships will do one of two things: They will propel you forward or they will pull you back. You have to make the choice every time. At the end of the day, my colleagues and

I believe everything important begins with culture. It defines us and how we work. It also defines the customer experience and, ultimately, it dictates the story about us people will tell.

NEXT STEPS

Define your values. What values form the backbone of your company? What qualities matter to you more than anything else, including a signed contract? What qualities make a potential client undesirable?

Examine your policies and procedures. How do you infuse your desired culture into your business? Do you have a screening system in place to ensure that you can build a cohesive team whose members are respectful of the company, its clients, and each other? How do you underline its importance in everything you do?

CHAPTER 8

GROWTH

THE FOUNDATION OF THE DOORPRENEUR MODEL

Being a Doorpreneur is a process, like anything else in serial entrepreneurship. To make your business both predictable and sustainable, you need to be *committed*, and that commitment needs to be ingrained in your DNA.

In this chapter, we'll examine some of the areas in which you can expand using property management as the cornerstone of your business, and I'll share some of the important lessons I've learned.

TIME TO DIVERSIFY

In 2013, my property management business was doing very well. Everything was firing on all cylinders. We ran our maintenance and cleaning functions in-house from the start so we had a good handle on that side of things, too.

I live in a community with just under 150,000 people so I began to get a little nervous about how much bigger we could grow the management business. As I considered new revenue streams, I thought about service providers with whom we were not happy and if that presented any opportunities. The answers were clear: landscaping and snow removal stood out above everything else.

Every season, we cringed at the difficulty we had with these services. Even though we were paying more than a quarter of a million dollars a year for them, our phones still rang with upset clients on the other end. The opportunity to step in ourselves was something that we could no longer ignore.

SIGNING ON THE DOTTED LINE

My partner and I talked about various possibilities and what it would look like to start another company. We knew we were not landscapers nor were we snow removal experts. The conversations were casual for the first few months, and then one day I saw a television program that changed the course of our business.

It was a TV series featuring CEOs going undercover to try to fix issues with their companies. This show, in particular, was about a landscaping business and I was intrigued. After watching the hour-long episode, I fell in love with the company that was featured, so I googled them as soon as the show was over.

What stood out for me was their overall look and feel. They did not look like the standard landscaper, and one scene stood out in particular. There were several employees working at a customer site. All of them were dressed the same in beautiful bright green and yellow uniforms that stood out. Their clean and shiny trucks gleamed from the street, and their manner seemed very calm yet efficient. They all knew what to do, how to do it, and how much time they had to do it. It was all very impressive, and I thought to myself that I would love to be part of exactly this type of company.

After some more research, I was shocked to find out that they were not too far away from where we were in Canada. Then I discovered that the company was a franchise, which meant we could essentially plug into the landscaping business and they would help us learn it.

Once I was sold on the idea of buying a landscaping franchise, I shared it with my business partner. After bringing him up to speed and giving him some time to do his own research, he also came to the same conclusion. Before we knew it, we were in discussions with one of the franchise sales associates and months later, we flew to their office to meet with the company owners.

The visit gave us a better understanding of the entire operation as well as the people behind the franchise, and it was a very big factor in us deciding to go the franchise route. We were very impressed with what we saw.

As we continued our research and due diligence, we were faced with something new and that was the issue of start-up capital. Luckily for us, our management company did not require a tremendous cash outlay when we started. We knew that was not the case with this venture if we decided to pursue it.

There was an initial cost to buy into the franchise and then start-up fees associated with acquiring all the essential equipment. Still, with our due diligence complete, we decided to take the plunge and buy the franchise. At the end of the day, I would say that the start-up process cost us about $100,000. In order to fund that, we used some cash savings and also got a loan from our local bank. They are known to have good interest rates for start-ups, and they were very helpful in getting us up and running in a short period of time.

Once we signed on the dotted line, we had another major decision to make: Who would run this new company for us? Up until then, both my partner and I were running the property management company. Bringing on a new company of this size was going to require one of us to work on it full time. We ultimately decided that my partner would run the new company and I would take over most responsibilities on the property management side. That said, we still had roles and responsibilities in both companies.

The start-up phase of the new company was new and exciting, and things went very well from the get-go. This is where the beauty of the Doorpreneur system comes into effect. We came into the franchise with an existing book of business from our management company, which allowed us to hit the ground running. The parent franchise company was happy because they had instant royalties coming in. That being said, we had no intention of servicing only our own property management business; we wanted to grow a big landscaping business and that meant expanding to the general public.

Just through word of mouth, we were quickly able to grow a book of business that kept us very busy. I would estimate that 50 percent of our work came from our own properties and the other 50 percent was from the public. Over the years, we've now reached a point where 85 percent of our business is from the public and only 15 percent from our management portfolio.

In order to grow this new business beyond our rent roll, our plan was to attend a local home show in early March 2014 in order to be ready for the upcoming summer season. Looking back now, this show was much more important for us than we could have imagined. We worked quickly and had a brand-new custom trailer in our booth along with other franchise-related material. We looked great and we stood out, which is exactly what we wanted to do.

At this show, two things happened. First, we met one of our biggest clients to date, even though we didn't know it at the time. It was a Saturday morning and he walked up to our booth, asked us a few questions, took one of our pamphlets, and then left.

A couple of weeks later, we heard from a man who said his boss had picked up one of our brochures and would like some quotes for landscaping. We later found out that his boss was the owner of one of the area's largest trucking companies. We were pretty excited, to say the least. We've been working with that company ever since and they have been amazing. They love and appreciate great landscaping, and we bend over backwards to make them happy.

The second thing that happened at the home show was that we met Kevin, a young man who ended up becoming our operations manager. He was looking for a change, and I think we could all feel a special relationship was in the making.

GRAB TALENT WHEN YOU FIND IT

My partner and I got into landscaping because we knew we could manage it, but we also knew we did not have the expertise to run a world-class operation. Kevin was an expert landscaper, exactly what we needed at the time. We had been looking for someone who knew the ins and outs of the business, could serve our clients well, and didn't just see the job as a summer gig. Kevin is still with us today and so is his wife and his father. They are the backbone of our company, and we would not be where we are if it were not for them.

That first summer in the landscaping business was interesting. We had a lot of our own clients and attracted many more. There also were days when we thought we had lost our minds. One of the biggest challenges was accounts receivable. We were used to running a business where we got paid first so we were not used to chasing customers for payments. (By the way, we still don't like this part, but it's part of that world.)

Another challenge had to do with the expenses associated with landscaping, which never seem to end. With everything from equipment purchases and equipment breakdowns to cracked windshields, I think we experienced it all that first year.

We were ecstatic when the season was over and looked forward to winter and snowplowing. Little did we know that winter is an entirely different beast when it comes to operations. When it snows, you have to be there immediately. This means there are long days and nights, cold weather, and missed holidays.

Our first winter was a nightmare with more than 500 centimeters of snow (the equivalent of 16.4 feet) within four months. We worked around the clock. I remember opening gifts with my children on Christmas morning and then going out to help shovel some properties because we were so far behind.

We did a lot of things wrong that year and Mother Nature was not kind to us, but we learned many valuable lessons and kept going.

HITTING OUR STRIDE

We're now in our fifth year of operations. We still make mistakes but we've gotten pretty good at what we do. We're not a huge company and we only cater to very specific clients. We're loyal to those who came on board early and always look to create long-lasting partnerships.

Owning a landscaping/snow removal business is not for everyone. It's a business where you need to be very hands on. You need to be out in the field with your staff on a regular basis to keep in constant contact with them. Keeping on top of the work and the time it takes to do the work is very important when it comes to time efficiencies. If a person takes an extra 10 minutes per site mowing a lawn up to 15 times a day, you can easily see how quickly this could be a problem over the course of a week.

The perfect owner for these businesses is someone who's not afraid to get his or her hands dirty and put in the work. It would also help to be mechanically inclined and a fan of big equipment and the outdoors. If this is you, it can be a great addition to your property management foundation. If this is not you, don't worry, there are many more businesses you can consider. Looking back, I would have preferred acquiring a smaller company so I could have had a better initial footing.

We got into some trouble early on in our landscaping company because we just wanted to get out there and didn't focus enough on price quotes. We were excited to have some money coming in, and to be honest, we had no idea how much you could lose if you didn't quote accurately. In order to effectively quote a job in most businesses, you must have a crystal clear sense of your costs, including labor, equipment, and overhead. For part of the first year, we made our best guesses, and unfortunately, we lost a lot of jobs.

It was a tough pill to swallow, but we learned a lot and have gotten a lot better over the years and have learned to rely on technology to take all the guesswork out of the process. Your costs typically are stored in the system, and all you do from there is input job details. The software then provides a number that includes your costs and desired profit margin.

START SLOW

To get the best results, I recommend you take your time with your first venture outside the rent roll. When you have resolved any problems and mastered serving your own properties, then you can reach out to new clients beyond your property management sphere. I recommend that you strategically handpick the people with whom you would like to work—people who love landscaping and, on the snow-clearing side of things, sites with as few complications as possible. A lot can go wrong when you have several feet of snow coming down in a matter of hours!

I have found it to be extremely helpful over the years to remember that I don't know everything about all businesses. As you grow your business empire as a Doorpreneur, don't be afraid to ask for help. Talk to people and listen when they have insights about areas in which you hope to expand.

It's true that the world is competitive, but it's equally true that many people are willing to give you a hand up if they know you respect them and appreciate the help.

NEXT STEPS

Do your research. Not only do you have to understand your current business but you must gather as much information as possible on the industry you want to join. Cast a wide net to research and talk to people who can tell you what it involves.

Be strategic. Identify specific opportunities that match your business goals and go after them. You'll establish a solid client base more quickly by being focused, and you can pick up additional business as you grow.

CHAPTER 9

TECHNOLOGY AND THE REINVENTION OF PROPERTY MANAGEMENT

I'm a tech geek at heart and always will be. It's served me well in my journey to becoming a Doorpreneur. When I hear about all the cool stuff that is being done in software these days, I get really excited. But sadly, I'm quickly reminded of how slowly software in the property management world has evolved.

We have a few giants in the property management software space that dominate the game, but unfortunately, they don't always play nicely with others, even though a capacity to integrate with other software tools is one of the most important features needed today.

If I take my consumer hat off and think like a software business owner, I understand the allure of wanting to keep data secure. If you read any new blog or article about tech companies, you'll surely hear that data is the new gold. Companies are able to mine this data and do all sorts of cool stuff with it. Think about a large property management software vendor and all the data they have on properties, rents, expenses, leasing, evictions, and maintenance— the list goes on and on.

Now, think of large financial institutions that are heavily invested in real estate. Do you think this data would be valuable to them to help them analyze deals, discover new trends among certain age groups, and determine how and when tenants turn to buyers? The possibilities are mind-boggling. So yes, data is the new gold if you know how to use it.

Software has the ability to help us be more efficient in our jobs or it can downright slow us down. I've put together an extensive list of software products that I use and have tried over the last 10 years. The point here is not to explain the pros and cons of each tool but to explain how tech can help you build and run a better property management business.

The nice thing is that there is tremendous overlap in property management software with almost any other business you'll add on your Doorpreneur journey since the basics—lead management, accounting, email, calendars, and marketing—are the same.

SOFTWARE RECOMMENDATIONS

Property management has distinct requirements, just like any other business. In addition to the normal, everyday tools like email, spreadsheets, and documents, there are many others that we need. At last count, we use well over 10 different programs on a daily basis in order to get our jobs done.

As of early 2019, here are my top recommended property management picks, in no particular order:

- Buildium (buildium.com)
- Property Ware (propertyware.com)
- Rent Manager (rentmanager.com)

- Appfolio (appfolio.com)
- Yardi (yardi.com)

All of these tools are comprehensive but do things differently. Most, if not all, of the vendors also provide free trial periods so you can test their product and determine what will work best for you. Overall feel and ease of use will be the most important criteria as you shop around for a solution.

OPERATIONS/COMMUNICATIONS

In addition to the management software, you are likely to spend most of your time with operations and communications software.

We use Google's G Suite for Business, which includes email, calendars, and Google Docs. Others prefer Outlook (Microsoft). Try them both to get a feel for what you prefer, but I think tools like Word and Excel are must-haves since most people use them.

When it comes to communication, we love Slack. It's a solid product, simple to use, and it's free! We use this for quick intercompany communications when email is not as effective.

We typically have a lot of property listings at any given time, which means we also work a lot on our website platform. WordPress sites are my go-to because they are well known in the tech community and you can find affordable talent to work on them.

Finally, there's Dropbox and other types of cloud-based storage. Since we are paying G Suite clients, we get access to Google Drive but I've never been a big fan. I've always been a Dropbox user, and it's still my preferred cloud storage software. We upgraded to the paid version for its security and are very happy with it.

Here are some useful links:

- Email/Calendar/Drive (gmail.google.com)
- Excel/Word (microsoft.com)
- Adobe Writer (adobe.com)
- Slack (slack.com)
- Dropbox (dropbox.com)
- Website Platform (wordpress.com)

CRM/LEAD MANAGEMENT

Most property management software companies do not provide Customer Relationship Management software (CRMs) or lead management platforms, but there are tons of companies out there that provide some really great CRM solutions. Some are free, and some are very expensive. As our businesses continue to grow and become more and more complex, the need for a great CRM and lead management tool also becomes increasingly important.

With today's technology, a lot of tasks can be automated, though I'm still a firm believer that face-to-face conversations are best. That being said, once a relationship has been established, automated content and touch points can provide incredible value for your business. I've tested all of the following platforms and nearly two dozen others.

I have yet to find the ultimate tool, and the ones that prove to be close to perfect are too expensive and require too much time and too many resources to fully integrate into my business. My advice is to start by setting up your own workflow and lead management processes in Excel, and once they're proven to work, find the tool that fits your specific needs best.

Here are some useful links:

- LeadSimple (leadsimple.com)
- Pipedrive (pipedrive.com)
- Podio (podio.com)
- HubSpot (hubspot.com)

SELF-SHOWING/MAINTENANCE

Self-showing software, which works with lock boxes, is all the rage. The allure of allowing prospects to book their own showings and not have to be there is quite enticing, to say the least. I have yet to do this because more than 90 percent of our showings are in units that are occupied and tenant coordination is required. That being said, we're in the process of working with one of these vendors to give it a try because I see the value of using it when possible.

Most property management software suites provide maintenance functionality. We've been using Buildium's built-in task management system and it's worked out fine. However, other third party tools are focused solely on maintenance, including Property Meld.

Here are some useful links:

- Rently (rently.com)
- Tenant Turner (tenantturner.com)
- Property Meld (propertymeld.com)
- ShowMojo (web.showmojo.com)

EMAIL MARKETING/FUNNELS

Let's shift the conversation now to one of my passions: Marketing! Reliable and effective communication with others is critical. One of my favorite tools is Mailchimp, which you can use to send out mass emails for free to your various constituencies. Our lists contain people whom we want to stay in front of, including property owners, tenants, and prospects.

Once you have your email list created, you can segment them into different groups. For example, you can create a sublist of owners who are interested in buying another property within the next 12 months. Or perhaps you want to create a sublist of tenants who are always late with their rent so you can be more proactive with reminders.

Once you've mastered the art of mass email, you can start looking at a new trend called funnels, which are automated chains of email marketing messages. Think of a funnel as a method of storytelling. For instance, when someone inquires about one of my properties, they get an automated message with a nicely crafted "thank you" and a video that features me telling them more about the company. The reactions have been overwhelmingly positive.

The other advantage of this system is that I get their email address and, with their permission, I can continue the conversation and send them regular communications so that I stay in the top of their mind. In other words, we're nurturing the relationship with both scheduled messages and real-time information and updates. This system alone will set you apart from most other management companies.

Here are some useful links:

- Mailchimp (mailchimp.com)

- Keap & Infusionsoft (keap.com)
- ActiveCampaign (activecampaign.com)
- ClickFunnels (clickfunnels.com)

GRAPHIC DESIGN

Graphic design can be pretty tough for a lot of people. Working with tight budgets as we all do, we need to be able to create graphics on our own as well as find alternative solutions to paying big design fees, especially when we have such diverse clients. Whether it's design for print or the web, there is always something needed.

Over the years, I've fallen in love with some online creative platforms that have enabled me to get things done quickly and cheaply. Fiverr is one. Prices start at five dollars but be prepared to up that a bit for more quality design. That being said, I've had some great success with it.

Another site is Canva.com, which allows virtually anyone to design something without a professional art background. It provides different templates for websites, flyers, and (my favorite) social media posts.

Here are some useful links:

- Fiver (fiverr.com)
- Upwork (upwork.com)
- Canva (canva.com)
- 99designs (99designs.com)

PROJECT MANAGEMENT

At any given time, we have 20 to 30 active projects, which typically involve maintenance, staff, or company issues and all of them need a place to live and breathe. I've tried to find the perfect software solution, and I've concluded it doesn't exist. We've ended up using Asana because it's fairly straightforward and it's free. I'm also a heavy user of Evernote for personal use.

Here are some useful links:

- Asana (asana.com)
- Evernote (evernote.com)
- Basecamp (basecamp.com)
- Trello (trello.com)

SO WHY AM I SUCH A TECHIE?

I didn't know how much I would fall in love with technology nor did I comprehend the impact it would have on my life and businesses. As a young man, when I abruptly quit my job at a local call center and went to study network administration, I knew I was interested in computer systems. But I didn't know the depth of my fascination.

One day in class, about two weeks into the course, my entire world changed. My instructor was up at the board showing us how to get access to one of the main servers in the school. He mentioned the name of the specific server and told us to wait a minute because we needed its IP address to obtain access, "192.169.2.1," I yelled out from memory.

The class went silent, and everyone stared at me. My instructor thanked me and gave me a nod in confidence. To this day, I have no idea how I remembered that strange set of numbers. I had learned what an IP address was only a week earlier, yet it stuck in my mind.

I had never been so in love with learning, and ever since then, I knew that computers would play a huge part in my life.

Two months before my graduation, a recruiting agency came to my school and interviewed some students for a job. I was one of the finalists and it was a heady experience for a kid like me. They flew me up to their headquarters for the day to do another interview and then offered me a job. I had never been on an airplane before or gone anywhere and here I was at the airport with a limousine waiting for me. The next thing I knew, the school had agreed to let me leave early with full credits and I was packing to move to Toronto, more than 1,200 miles away from home.

After a couple of months of settling into my new life, I saw some opportunities to learn some new technologies and possibly move into a more prestigious role. With that in mind, I enrolled in a night course at a local college. It wasn't long before a coworker told me that a hot tech company was hiring. After a year of working for the employer that gave me my first opportunity, I left to pursue what was a better job with higher pay.

Platform Computing was a privately held software company that began in 1992 in Toronto with headquarters in Markham and 11 branch offices across the US, Europe, and Asia. Its revenue in 1993 was approximately $300,000 and it spiraled to $12 million by 2003. (It was eventually purchased by IBM in 2012.) I worked there as a technical consultant from 2000 to 2014, and it was an exciting place to be. I was a quick learner and happy as a computer geek, continuing to see myself and my life develop and mature.

I was able to stay with the firm when I moved back to my hometown in 2006 and began a family with the birth of my daughter, Sara, and my son, Caden. I travelled the world and got to work with some of the biggest companies around the globe. The pay was fantastic, and the people with whom I worked were world class. I excelled at my job and was promoted several times over in nearly 15 years with the company.

The technology world was so good to me that you might be surprised I left it. But life has a way of taking you to late night discussions around campfires with friends and you wake up with a resolve to change your course again. I ultimately felt unfulfilled and knew that, as exhilarating as this work was, I was not living up to my true potential.

In my personal book of life, I believe we are here for a reason and not fulfilling your potential is a sin. I knew that an entrepreneurial spirit burned within me. I would have to set it free if I were going to be happy and do the work I was intended to do. When I did make the jump into property management and then into other businesses, I took with me the knowledge that whatever I did could be greatly enhanced with the proper application of technology.

NEXT STEPS

Simplify your business process and procedures. Have you identified your endgame? Focus on it, and review every aspect of your business. Are the steps you are taking today leading you to where you want to be tomorrow? Or, are you mired in mental clutter and not looking beyond next month? You can change your mindset now and make life easier for yourself.

Incorporate technology. Are you limping along on an outdated system or using what you inherited from somebody else? Consider software solutions that can streamline your processes. Technology is one of the best investments you can make because of the time it frees up for you to address other areas of business growth.

CHAPTER 10

GROW EVERY DAY

People who knew me as a young man wouldn't believe how inspired I am to learn today. And if there's one regret I have in my life, it's that I waited so long to take my self-development seriously. What I want to tell you is that it's never too late to work on yourself and maximize your potential.

I wasn't much of a student; I only did the minimum to get by. Sometimes, I cut it a little too close. I still have the occasional nightmare about failing French my junior year in high school and having to take it all over again in summer school. It was an eye-opening experience to realize that my lack of attention could cost me what I really wanted, which was to graduate with my friends and make my mother proud. Even so, it took a couple more years before I discovered that education could be invigorating and immensely satisfying.

From podcasts to books and lectures, I always find ways to expand my knowledge base and seek practical applications. I use my car as my own personal university and am always listening to some kind of educational material. With today's technology, everything you need to continue learning is available at your convenience if you use your time wisely.

My newly acquired expertise always pays off for my clients and my own sense of fulfillment. When I provide excellent service to tenants in our buildings, and they are happy and comfortable, I know I am enhancing their quality of life. That makes me happy. When I create wealth for property owners and they are pleased with the investments, this also makes me happy. When I learn new ways to challenge myself and turn what I know into other businesses, that makes me happy. And if I can help other business owners do the same, it gives me joy.

THE 5 AM CLUB

In 2013, the year before I left my successful computer career, I was in a bad place. Just stuck in a rut, or the "pit," as I call it now. I wasn't happy with how my life was going. I knew I had the capacity to do much more but I didn't know how to unlock it.

The stars must have been aligned because a friend of mine reached out to me around that time. We met for lunch and he surprised me with a copy of the bestselling book *The Leader Who Had No Title* by Robin Sharma. I had no idea who Robin Sharma was but dove into the book that night. It's hard to put into words but I felt one of those "aha!" moments when something just all of a sudden makes sense.

Robin is amazing at telling stories and folding them into life lessons that tug at your heart. In this book, he told a beautiful story about how to operate as a human being and it touched my heart. It was so simple yet so foreign to me. Once I opened up to the possibilities, I was all in and quickly bought all his other books. I was hooked.

One of his most well-known concepts is "The 5 AM Club" and it particularly stood out to me. The idea is simple: You get up at 5:00

a.m. to work on yourself for an hour. You exercise part of the time and then you read, meditate, and plan your day. I was consistently amazed by what I could accomplish in an hour. Some days, I even got up at 4:30 a.m. because I was so excited to have time alone to work on "me."

(When his new book, *The 5 AM Club: Own Your Morning, Elevate Your Life,* came out in 2019, I was like a child waiting to open presents on Christmas morning. I could not put it down, and it rebooted my desire to get back into my early morning routine, which had become a little stale. It gave me the nudge I needed.)

It's not always easy to get up early, and I've learned over the years that I cannot function well without proper sleep. When I get up so early, I can become a zombie by dinnertime and I'm usually in bed by 9:00 p.m. In order to get up early consistently, I sometimes have to sleep in to give my body what it needs to recover. Sometimes you just have to slow down to go faster. This is definitely the case for me when it comes to sleep.

EDUCATION LEADS TO GROWTH

When I took that time for myself, I often was able to reflect on my industry from another perspective. I realized that if we look at property managers and realtors, a major gap exists in their comparative levels of formal education and professional training. A realtor must study and pass an exam to secure a license. Many of them invest in additional sales courses and seminars to stay on top of trends in their industry and learn to be the best that they can be.

Most property managers are left to learn on our own, and the harsh reality is the majority of us will never do anything to advance our skills.

We'll just learn on the job and leave it at that. But I know now, and I believe passionately, that we need to learn every day if we really want to be the best at our business and grow our property management firms into Doorpreneurship empires.

Why aren't we building and sharing knowledge? Why aren't we getting together and pushing the technology industry to meet our needs? Why are we working in isolation when there are so many of us? Part of this has to do with how we are largely viewed in a negative context.

One of Sharma's big questions is: "What are you doing to help build a new and better world?" He encourages us to write lists of what we don't like about our industries or our organizations or our lives. Then he recommends that we set out to improve those things. Start small or go big, it doesn't matter, he says. Just do something.

Inspired by his teaching, I try to incorporate new ideas into my work, and I keep records of what succeeds and what fails and what I learn at each stage of the process. One of the first things I learned is that running a property management business with 50 units is very different from running hundreds or even thousands of units.

For example, when I started my management company, it was a one-man show. I grew to more than 50 units pretty quickly and realized that I needed some technological assistance to help manage everything. I started with Microsoft Excel as I'm sure 99 percent of property managers do, and I used it for my property details as well as a very basic accounting system. The rapid growth of my business soon put an end to that.

I threw myself 100 percent into property management software to learn everything I could, whether it was listening to podcasts, reading white papers, or spending a lot of time testing the various tools. The process in itself was quite fun and insightful as I not only learned more about my industry specific software but also learned a lot more about property management in general.

Another big shift for me was the overall mindset that I needed to have in order to handle everyone for whom I was responsible. To work a full-time job, raise a young family, and start a new business, you need to become quite good at time management, and author Stephen Covey's time management matrix in *The 7 Habits of Highly Effective People* became my go-to strategy.

It taught me to focus on what's important and what's not. I find this strategy particularly helpful in the property management space because we often get bombarded with other people's agendas, and we need to make the most of the little time we have to work on what else is important and needs our attention.

I've also learned that, as a property manager, you must master skills in marketing, financing, and leadership, and all of these skills can be transferred to the other businesses you create.

I understand that knowledge and expertise helps ease the pressure of the situations in which I find myself, and since some learning also comes from *doing*, I push myself constantly to try new things. Every time I apply a new skill to my companies, they change and become more efficient and profitable.

If you want to use your property management business as the basis to become a Doorpreneur, you have no choice but to continually learn and grow or you will never be able to pull it off.

DEFY THE LIMITS

The average property management company in Canada and the US manages between 300 and 500 doors but they rarely get any bigger because it's tough to get there and tough to stay. The reality of the situation is that if you can't inspire yourself to progress and grow, you will get to the point where your profits start to decline or plateau.

Unless you live and work in one of the world's mega-cities where new apartments go up every week, you'll ultimately come to the physical limits of your client base. Even when you branch out to other cities, you'll hit walls, too. But that doesn't mean you need to stop growing.

If you can generate maintenance, cleaning, landscaping, and snow removal as multimillion-dollar spin-offs of your property management business, it's okay if one of your revenue streams hits a limit. You can still expand the others and find new ones. You just need to take time to imagine the possibilities and acquire the skills to make them a reality.

But to do that, you have to appreciate this industry as a good one with skillful, well-intentioned people providing comfortable homes to millions of people around the world and creating wealth and protecting investments for millions of others. This is nothing for which we should hide under a rock—it's a business to be proud of. Today, I share the love and appreciation for what I do with everyone around me.

In the beginning, I am sure people laughed at me when I wasn't looking or thought that I was a little nuts. Yet, slowly but surely, I sense people are beginning to see a different side of being a property manager. They're shifting their perspective of the industry as a whole and growing in their respect for seeing it as the foundation for many related businesses, including landscaping, snow removal, maintenance companies, sales, etc. In other words, they are witnessing the birth of the Doorpreneur.

At the end of the day, the amount of time and energy you put into learning and growing yourself will be magnified 100 times over in the way you run and grow your businesses. Don't wait for the industry to offer you everything you need to know on a silver platter. Instead, learn something new each day and then share it, and before you know it, the level of expertise will rise and the image of our industry will begin to shine.

MY GO-TO PODCASTS

Over the years, I've become a huge fan of podcasts, especially since I'm in the car so much. I'm an Apple guy so that's where I get my content. Some shows contain quick tidbits of information that are very actionable, and other podcasts provide longer form interviews with one golden nugget after another.

I'm a big believer in listening and learning from those in your own industry, but I also love learning from people who are killing it elsewhere. This is where you can pick up strategies that perhaps nobody ever thought of implementing in your industry.

Here are some of the podcasts that I listen to today:

- BiggerPockets Real Estate Investing & Wealth Building
- Smart Passive Income (Pat Flynn, a bit of everything)
- Bulletproof Executive Radio (Dave Asprey, Biohacker)
- The MFCEO Project (Andy Frisella)
- Warrior Week (Sam Falsafi)
- Marketing School (Neil Patel and Eric Siu)

- Profitable Property Management (Jordon Muela)
- The #DoorGrowShow (Jason Hull)

I have to continually remind myself that listening to content for the sake of listening and passing time is one thing but using that information is totally different. To help with this, I've implemented a daily strategy—"Discover and Declare"—that forces me to act on what I learn. The idea is that you learn something new and then you teach what you just learned to someone else. It's an incredibly powerful exercise that forces you to absorb content with intent but it's not always easy. This is where you truly learn, not in the reading or listening but in the teaching or declaring.

The teaching part can start as simple as sharing a social media post about what you learned, talking to your staff about it, teaching it to your kids, or even just taking a video of yourself teaching yourself! Knowing that you have to teach it to someone else will force you to learn it at a different and often deeper level. Try it, and be sure to tag #Doorpreneur on LinkedIn, Facebook, or Instagram.

NEXT STEPS

Learn something new. If you can't remember when you last did this, then it's time to push yourself to read blogs, or listen to podcasts, or go to seminars and work on self-development. In turn, as your knowledge base grows, you will find new ways to adapt what you know to growing your business.

Make a list. Write down 10 new experiences you will enjoy in the next 90 days. You don't have to drastically alter your life but as busy as you are, you need to set aside priority time to engage in new experiences. That's true even if they are just small steps to expand your mind.

CHAPTER 11

INVEST IN YOU!

A solid morning ritual is one of the greatest gifts we can give ourselves, and I'm blessed that I was taught its importance many years ago. With the 5:00 a.m. routine under my belt, I go into each day wearing a coat of can-do armor that nobody can pierce.

Too many people today hide under the covers, scared to make changes in their lives. They're scared to do the hard work and face their fears, stuck in their daily grind and not knowing where or how to start. However, if there is one thing I've learned over the last five years, it's that I'm worth an investment of time, money, and energy. This is the message everyone needs if they switch up their lives and become Doorpreneurs.

A PASSION FOR PREPARATION

I was 16 years old when I picked up my first dumbbell. Little did I know it would lead to an entire decade of intense, focused concentration on bodybuilding and eventually lead me to Canada's top national competition. That experience—from intense workouts to strict diets—taught me the power of discipline, which has carried over into my work as a property manager.

Bodybuilding taught me how important it was to stay focused and be willing to put in the work. You can't be a player if you are not willing to work hard to be in peak condition, and you can't take shortcuts.

Taking care of myself as a bodybuilder also taught me a great deal about being successful in business. If I want to accomplish something, I always ask myself if I am willing to properly prepare for it. Are my expectations in line with what I know I have to do to accomplish my goals?

If you want to be a Doorpreneur, you can't sit there and hope that new businesses will fall into your lap. You have to prepare for it, just as the bodybuilder prepares for competition. You need to bring in a steady stream of new clients, and to that end, I've cultivated relationships with investors for years. Some I take out for lunch or coffee. Others I call on a regular basis so they keep me in mind. I also got my realtor's license so I can be part of that world, too. My strategies didn't pay off in a week or even a month. My expectations are set for many years and it works.

Each quarter, I also plan how many additional units I intend to bring into my firm. I plan out my weeks for the next three months so I know whom I will talk to and how I will implement various marketing initiatives to reach my goals.

Getting new clients is a function of sales. You need to get out there and talk to people, develop relationships, and position yourself as an expert in your field. Then you need to be able to close the deal. You can have all the passion in the world for business but you can't grow businesses until your passion for preparation equals or exceeds your passion for growth.

Five years ago, I was introduced to a new way of planning and setting goals called 90-Day Challenges. Creating longer term plans are tough for me because so much change happens, but I still like to have a general idea of where I'm going. A 90-day target gives me the ability to get things done, quickly gain momentum, and stack up some wins.

I like to keep the process of creating a 90-day challenge as simple as possible. I set various targets for different things in my life, but I'll stick to business for this example since I always plan for growth. I used to measure growth in terms of door count, but I've recently changed this to income—more specifically, net profit.

If I'm looking to add an additional $100,000 in net profit to my business over the next 90 days, I need to be able to break that down into several components. First, I need to start by understanding why I want this to happen. Making more money is one thing but asking why makes it that much more powerful because it adds a larger sense of purpose. The next step is to start thinking about potential obstacles, which can be tougher to put on paper, especially if this is something new to you.

Once you've gotten past these two steps, you can start to reverse engineer your target. In other words, you can break up the target into smaller chunks of 30-day and 60-day benchmarks. If my target is to add $100,000, maybe the first 30 days are all about creating leads, filling the pipelines, and turning these leads into real prospects. The next 60 days are all about executing and closing.

Each week, I go through the same exercise to keep tabs on where I'm at within the challenge. Sunday mornings or nights are my planning times when I map out my week as well as reflect on the prior week in order to make any adjustments to my plan. The session starts with figuring out one main task that I need to accomplish, along with four supporting activities to help me accomplish that main task and get me closer to my end goal.

THE INTRODUCTION OF WARRIOR

During one of my morning power hour sessions, I happened to be responding to a friend on Facebook who was doing some pretty cool stuff as part of the Wake Up Warrior Movement.

The movement, founded by former real estate mogul Garrett J. White, has completely transformed my life in every way. After I watched an online sales pitch for the Warrior Experience, I watched video after video for more than two hours. I laughed, and I cried. I could not believe what I was seeing. For the first time in my life, I was listening to someone who felt what I was feeling and thought what I thought. It was like he knew me better than I did.

The advertising was brilliant but also honest and true. White was an entrepreneur, divorced, with three kids, and trying to find his way through this world. He had been through the same struggles as me and created this program to help other men get through some really tough times.

As soon as I was done watching the sales material, I booked a call with Garrett to attend Warrior Week. The program involved a week of training in California to help equip me with the tools to be able to overcome my barriers and live a full life. Our call was quick and to the point. All I needed to know was the cost and when I had to be there. Other than that, I was in!

We had two weeks of virtual coaching before the main event, and over those two weeks, my mind was opened up to new ways of thinking. When I arrived, Garrett greeted me and the first thing I was asked was, "Why are you here?" This question, so simple in nature, was excruciating to answer. I was all over the place, I knew I needed help but didn't really know what that help looked like.

Our first day at Warrior Week was physical with three workouts (called evolutions) to kick the living daylights out of us and break us down so that they could see the "real" us. They wanted to know how we dealt with pain and what we used as our "why" to help us get through the day.

I have always been a pretty fit guy, and the workouts for me were amazing, challenging, and a ton of fun. We did a traditional workout in the gym, CrossFit style, and then we hit the beach. Not only were we doing a workout but we also did some challenges involving grappling. I was in my element right up until I had to get in a boxing ring and fight another man! I knew this part of the experience was coming but I just did not know when. As we arrived at the location for our next "workout," I was nervous. I had not boxed since I was a kid and had no idea how things would turn out. We went through a number of talks before we ultimately got in the ring.

Things got pretty real in the moment I knew I was about to get punched in the face. As soon as the referee gave us the go-ahead, it was on. Punches were all over the place. My opponent hit me, I hit him, and this went on for three minutes. I remember saying to myself that this was not so bad. I didn't quit, and I didn't get knocked out.

It was three minutes of pure aggression, a primal release that they wanted us to feel and one that men should connect to on a regular basis. We need and crave it, yet most of us shy away from it. I walked away from the fight with a bloody nose and a ton of insights about myself. I was grateful for the experience and it is one that I will never forget. The day finished pretty late into the night. I was done. Exhausted by the physicality of the day and from the emotional toll it had on me, I was looking forward to a good night's sleep.

Day Two was focused on the concept of "being" in terms of our spirituality and mindfulness. This was uncharted territory for me. The morning started with a meditation session, something that I had never done before. One of the most memorable things I learned was a simple mantra-based technique that I still do to this day. Most men out there (and women as well) don't take much time to stop and just be still to take time and reflect. We don't give ourselves a break from the chaos of our lives and take time to go deep into ourselves. The gift of meditation is one of the most powerful gifts of my Warrior journey.

Day Three focused on "balance," looking at our relationships, and most important, our marriages and children. Throughout the week, we all had opportunities to share what we were going through and how we were feeling. This topic was quite sensitive to me but I jumped right in and it got messy quick! I was an emotional wreck for most of the day, and the other guys gave me the platform and the space to just get it out. The trainers were amazing at asking the right questions at the right times to help guide me through the areas that I needed to work on. It was transformational. I again learned many tools, including *The Work* by Byron Katie, that I could use going forward.

Our last day was all about business, and the point was that to be successful in business, one needs to be on point in the other three areas of our lives: Body, Being, and Balance. I'll be honest, I was not at Warrior for my business. I was there to regain my sanity. That being said, I was still pretty pumped to have some time working on some business ideas and strategies, working according to the 90-day sprints I previously mentioned.

By Day Four, we were all on fire and on point to crush our day. We went through a number of different talks and exercises, all of which taught us techniques for sales, marketing, planning, and execution. What seemed so complicated going into Warrior was like a walk in the park once we left the headquarters that night. Each of us left with a plan, the internal power to make it happen, and access to a brotherhood of men willing to go through hell and back to help support us.

I got exactly what I wanted from Warrior, and I'm not even sure if I can put it all into words. It opened my eyes to a whole new world of operating as a man. I feel as though I was running on autopilot before, letting my days control me without any idea how to control them. I returned home a new man—not a perfect man but a new and better version of me. I now know how I'm wired and what makes me tick and have the tools to deal with just about any situation. The only one who can get in my way now is me.

Most entrepreneurs I know don't spend enough time working on themselves. They have no place in their schedule for stillness and self-reflection, but I find my early morning routine provides me with clarity. It gives me the inner calm that I need to be productive and be the best version of myself.

Every day, I take at least 20 minutes to meditate and read something that will enlighten me spiritually and then I write in my journal about it. Meditation is one of the newer practices I have incorporated into my life. I also schedule small retreats away from my office to think deeply about my next steps in business and in life. These times are just as important as other appointments on my calendar. I often do this by working from home since our office is hectic and it's difficult to get uninterrupted time.

Initially, I didn't think I could calm myself enough to meditate but I had a breakthrough. I would often get in bed at night and just lie there for more than an hour, replaying my day and thinking about the next day, week, and year. But one night I just started saying my mantras and before I knew it, I was waking up the next morning. I thought it was a coincidence but when I tried it again the next night, I was asleep in minutes.

That is when I became a believer in the power of meditation. If I don't get away and think deeply on a regular basis, I don't feel the same, and I don't produce the same.

As you take care of yourself, also be sure to reach out to the people who help make your life worth living. Every day, I send a text to special people in my life and tell them I love and appreciate them. It is important to ensure that those who are close to you in your life know how much they mean to you. This fills their hearts and yours.

CARE FOR YOURSELF

Today, I understand the strength and energy I need to grow my businesses. I'm conscious of nutrition and what goes into my body and, as of the writing of this book, I'm in the process of preparing for my first Ironman in August 2019. My motto is: "You should sweat every day."

Taking care of our bodies is a great foundation for everything else around us. When we look and feel good, we tend to do better in just about everything. Neglecting ourselves isn't an option.

NEXT STEPS

Review your morning habits. What rituals start your day? Are they habits that boost your confidence and send you out into the world with a positive mindset? Do you look after your body with proper nutrition and exercise? Remember that you need to take care of yourself first or else you will never be able to fully take care of others.

Find space for contemplation. Do you find time to think deeply? What works for me may or may not work for you. I encourage you to find the space in every day to think deeply about what is important to you. Without that, you won't be able to achieve your top goals in work or life.

CHAPTER 12

THE MEANING OF SUCCESS

Whenever I pick up a self-help book or go on a retreat, I am asked whether I feel my work has purpose and fits into the broader meaning of my life. After all, what is the point of striving to be good at something if there's no meaning in it?

I'm not a self-development guru who has a pat answer to these questions. I'm a Doorpreneur trying to figure it all out. Some days, it feels like I'm running up against a wall, and other days, I feel like I'm making a real difference.

My first goal was to create the biggest property management company in my town, and I have accomplished that. My second goal was to do the same thing in the Maritimes, and I think we're there. Now my ultimate goal, and purpose in life, is to take all that I've learned and share it on a global stage.

In my heart, I think property managers play a significant role in the entire real estate cycle, even if we often are among the lowest paid with the hardest job. If it were not for us, properties would go downhill until everyone's homes and investments fell apart.

To me, property management not only is a strong and viable business in itself, doing important work, and creating value and wealth but it also is the foundation for being a Doorpreneur and an industry leader.

We all have to have faith that the work we do on this planet matters, and you and I are no exception.

THE QUINTESSENTIAL DOORPRENEUR

Today, I have become a serial entrepreneur who has property management as the foundation of my growing empire, and I'm hoping that the concept of being a Doorpreneur will grow as more and more people in the business realize its potential. The way I speak to a client today in that role is much different from the way I used to talk to them. I can now very clearly demonstrate and position myself and my company as the experts for anything property-related, indoors and outdoors.

So many opportunities exist for people who run a great business and provide wonderful service. People want to hire people whom they like and trust, and that is the ultimate responsibility of the Doorpreneur.

Build a class of brands that take everything to the next level. Create partnerships with your clients so that you can serve them in many facets and for many years. Take a holistic approach to everything and make sure everyone wins, your clients and you. The time has never been more right to review how our industry is perceived in the public eye and to improve and change its image. As baby boomers and millennials, the country's largest population groups, seek rental properties for their own unique reasons, ensuring these units are clean and well maintained and making them feel at home will be of paramount importance.

If you are currently in the business of property management, you have tremendous potential to grow and evolve. If you are not in the business and decide that it could be your calling, you can use this book as a guide to thinking about the industry differently and getting off on the right foot from the start.

To help guide your journey, here are my 15 rules for successful Doorpreneurship:

1. Build your core property management business first and ensure that it is sustainable before you do anything else. If you try to start 10 businesses all at once, they'll fail.

2. Position your company to control assets. That puts you in a position to engage with opportunities.

3. Be transparent. You have to first build a company of value within the property management framework and gain the trust of clients before you explore expansion.

4. Remember that property management is not a money grab or an easy way to build an empire. It's a tough business where you create value, and once you have accomplished that, you can offer more value with other companies.

5. Your secondary businesses should always generate the bulk of their revenue from *outside* clients. If your main property management company is feeding 100 percent of the clients to the secondary company, it's not a separate business. It's simply a service provided within the management company.

6. Keep your roles and responsibilities clear. Ensure a separation of your companies by sending your best managers to handle them.

7. You have to get jobs done right at the right price to succeed. When you start secondary businesses from your main property management business, you cannot take it for granted that you'll get the work.

8. Keep your core company strong to support the other companies. Save money by using the same office and accounting personnel. Each business is separate but still must be connected to the original framework.

9. Build a strong infrastructure before you branch out. Use what you know. With your property management firm, you already have business strategies and processes that can be applied to your other businesses.

10. Time management is crucial. Plan, delegate, dump, and outsource as needed. Do a little bit for each business every day. My partner and I, for instance, start every morning with a quick exchange of issues before reviewing prospects and sales.

11. Review the finances of your property management firm every month, according to its regular rental cycle. Review seasonal businesses like landscaping and snow-clearing more frequently.

12. Delegate (you can't do it all), and trust your team to do their jobs. Otherwise, you'll burn out. You cannot be the general manager of 10 different businesses. It's okay to branch out small as long as you think big, and you can incubate a business with one or two employees.

13. Create new brands as you go and expand. You don't want too many services within the same company.

14. Ask for help and guidance when you need it. Seek out mentors and individuals with industry experience when you can.

15. Remember anyone can be a Doorpreneur, building an empire of businesses on the foundation of property management, and helping to change an entire industry for the future.

NEXT STEPS

Reevaluate your potential. If you're already a property manager, take time now to consider which segments of your company have the potential to stand on their own and expand into new markets not currently within reach. If you are just thinking about going into property management, consider it as the foundation of your future business empire, not necessarily an end in itself.

Consider where your skills can take you. Think about how you get better and better at what you do. What is your ultimate goal? How can you take what you know and apply it to build a better business, and in turn, new businesses? How can you grow yourself into a Doorpreneur?

Made in the USA
San Bernardino, CA
11 November 2019